I0449499

A GUIDE

TO

REAGENTS IN ORGANIC SYNTHESIS

Dr. Sapana Gupta

(Seth Phool Chand Agrawal Smriti College, Nawapara Rajim, CG India)

Vinod Jena

(Government College Sarona Kanker, CG India)

&

Dr. R. S. Dhundhel

(Department of Chemistry, SSIPMT, Raipur, CG India)

LP Inc. Publisher North Carolina, USA
2015

Although great care has not been taken to provide accurate and current information, neither the author nor the publisher, nor anyone else associated with this publication, shall be liable for any loss, damage, or liability directly or indirectly caused or alleged to be caused by this book. The material contained herein is not intended to provide specific advice or recommendations for any specific situation

Copyright ©2015 by Dr. Sapana Gupta All rights reserved

This book or any portion thereof may not be reproduced or used in any manner whatsoever without the express written permission of the publisher except for the use of brief quotations in a book review or scholarly journal.

First Printing: 2015

ISBN: 978-1-329-16214-3

DEDICATION

To our friends all over the world

Thank you all.

Without your support and patience, we would have never achieved our dream.

ACKNOWLEDGMENTS

I would like to thank my teachers, my editor, my classmates, and my all friends all over the world whose suggestions guide me to complete this book.

CONTENTS

GILMAN REAGENT

It is a lithium and copper (diorganocopper) reagent compound, R_2CuLi, where R is an organic radical. It react with organic chlorides, bromides, and iodides to replace the halide group with an R group. This is extremely useful in creating larger molecules from smaller ones.

$$\begin{array}{c} R \\ \diagdown \\ \underset{\diagup}{C}u \ominus \oplus Li \\ R \end{array}$$

$$\left[R-Cu-R\right]^- Li^+ + R'-X \longrightarrow \left[\begin{array}{c} R' \\ | \\ R-Cu-R \\ | \\ X \end{array}\right]^- Li^+ \longrightarrow R-Cu + R-R' + Li-X$$

Ex 1

Ex 2

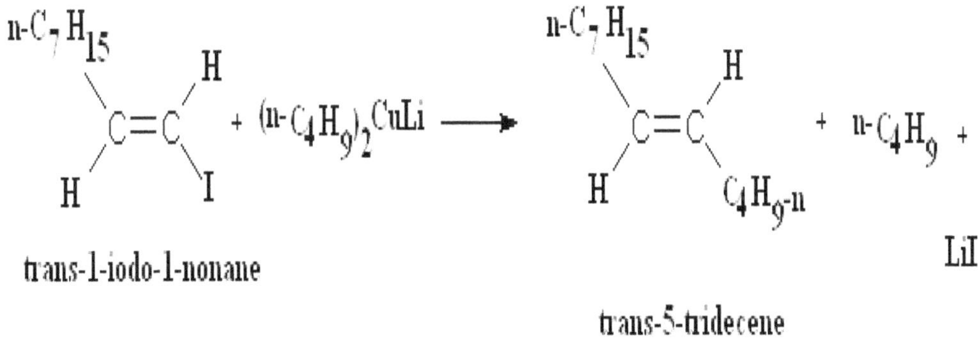

n-C7H15
H
C=C
H
I
+ (n-C4H9)2CuLi
n-C7H15
H
C=C
H
C4H9-n
+ n-C4H9 +
LiI
trans-1-iodo-1-nonane
trans-5-tridecene

Ex 3

$$R_2CuLi + R'X \longrightarrow R-R' + RCu + LiX$$

Ex 4

$$(C_6H_5)_2CuLi + ICH_2(CH_2)_6CH_3 \xrightarrow{\text{diethyl ether}} C_6H_5CH_2(CH_2)_6CH_3$$

Ex 5

$$(CH_3)_2CuLi + CH_3(CH_2)_8CH_2I \xrightarrow[0^\circ C]{\text{diethyl ether}} CH_3(CH_2)_8CH_2CH_3$$

Ex 6

1) $(CH_3CH_2)_2CuLi$

2) H_3O^+

Ex 7

1) R_2CuLi

2) H_3O^+

Ex 8

THF, -78 to 0 °C

4

Ex 9

α, β- unsaturated aldehyde or ketone

Gilman reagent

Product with alkyl group added at β- position

Ex 10

$(CH_3)_2CuLi$

THF, -78°C

Ex 11

a. Et_2CuLi

Et_2O, –78 °C

b. NH_4Cl, H_2O

Ex11

Ex 13

Organocuprates undergo 1,2-additions to aldehydes, ketones,and imines. Reactions are often highly diastereoselective

In bicyclic system below, addition is chemoselective, involving the. The reaction is also less hindered double bond of the dienone and stereoselective in that introduction of the "Me" group occurs preferentially from the less hindered side of the molecule.

Ex 14

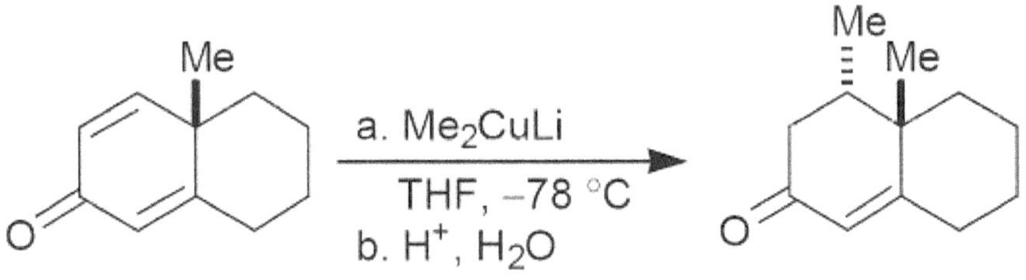

Me
a. Me2CuLi
THF, −78 °C
b. H+, H2O
Me
Me
O
O

Ex 15

O
a. n-Bu2CuLi
b. CH3I
c. NH4Cl, H2O
O
CH3
n-Bu

Ex 16

O
H3C
a. (CH3)2CuLi
Et2O, −78 °C
b. NH4Cl, H2O
O
H3C
CH3
95%
+
O
H3C
CH3
5%

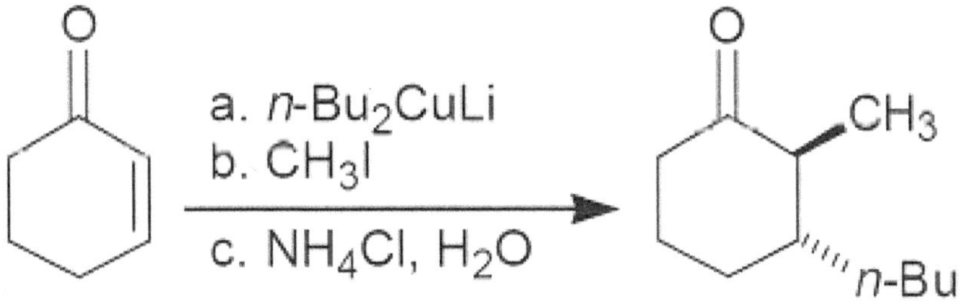

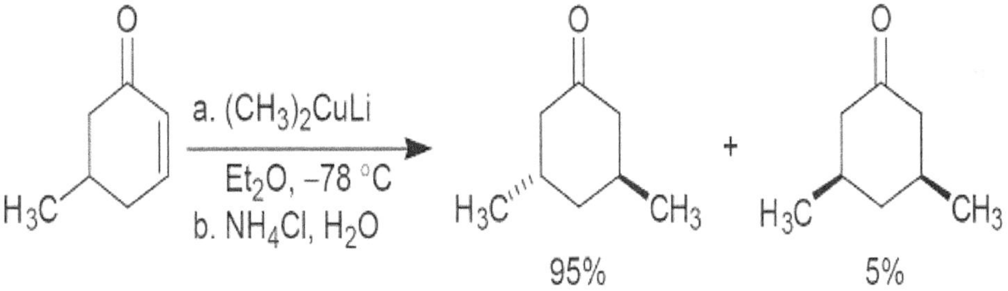

Ex 17

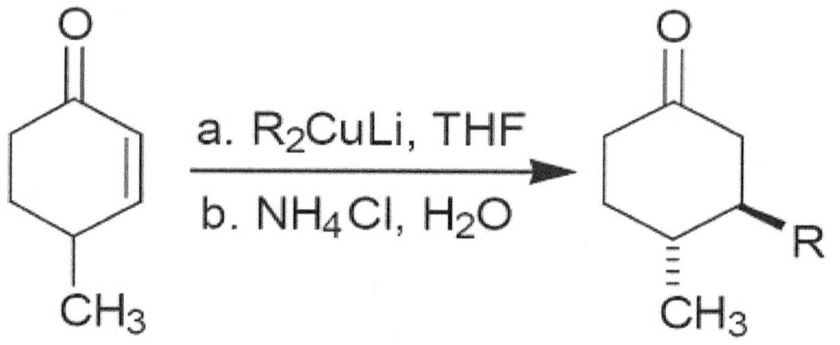

a. R2CuLi, THF
b. NH4Cl, H2O
CH3
R
CH3

Ex 18

i (n-Bu)2CuLi
ii CH3I
iii H+/H2O
O− Li+
n-Bu
CH3
n-Bu

Ex 19

R2CuLi, H3O+
R
H

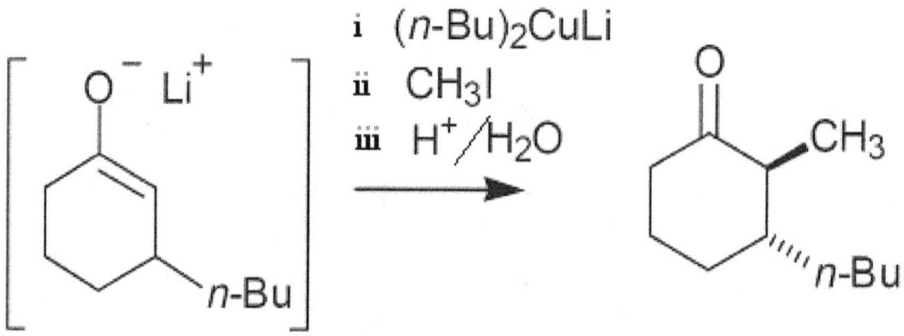

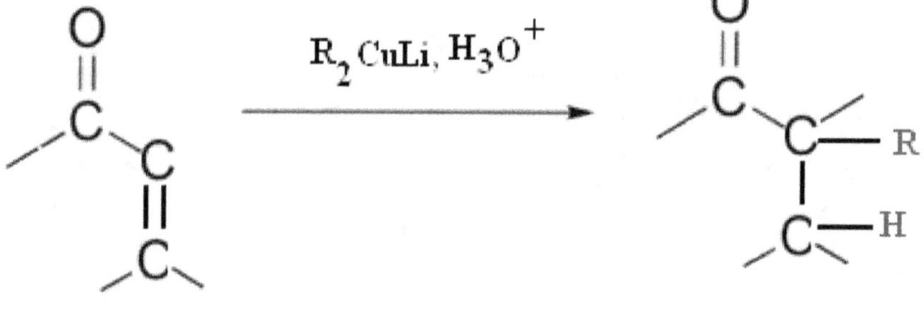

Ex 20

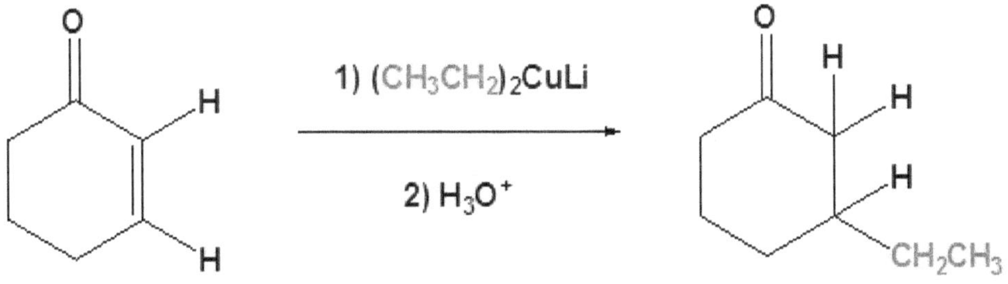

O
H
H
1) (CH3CH2)2CuLi
2) H3O+
O
H
H
H
CH2CH3

Ex 21

O
H3C
C
Cl
(CH3CH2)2CuLi
-78ºC
O
H3C
C
CH2CH3

Ex 22

Br
Br
+
Me2CuLi
Me
Me

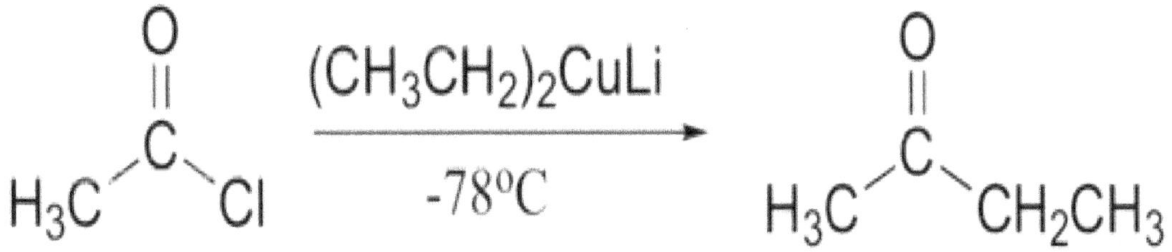

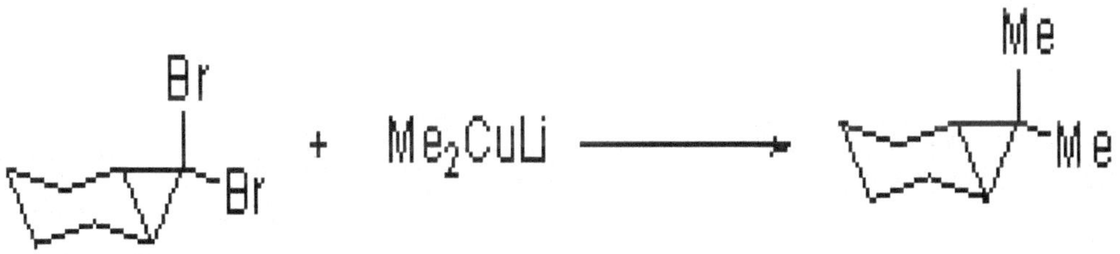

Ex 23

Ex 24

Ex 25

10

Ex 26

Ex 27

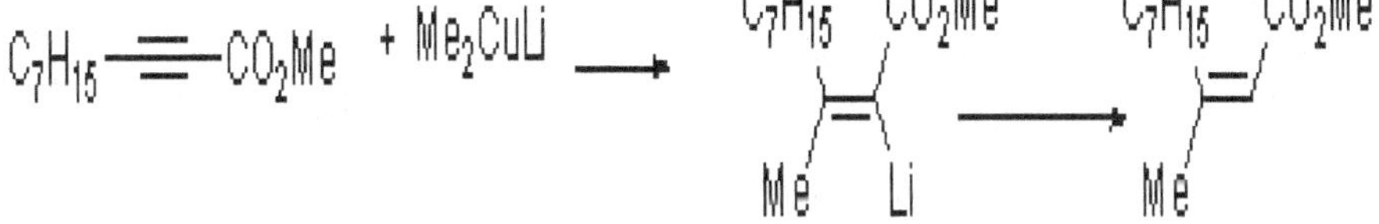

Epoxide opening with organocuprates is highly selective for the less hindered position. Substitution takes place with complete inversion of configuration at the electrophilic carbon. Epoxide reacts with organocopper reagents at the least substituted carbon atom to provide the corresponding alcohol.

Ex 28

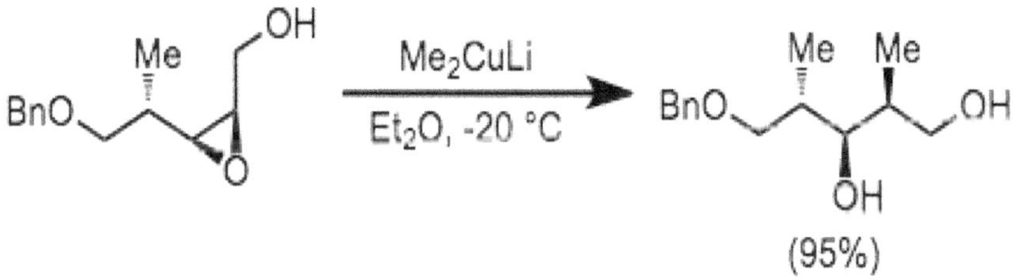

Ex 29

Ex 30

Ex 31

1,4-addition

12

Ex 32

Ex 33

Ex 34

Ex 35

Ex 36

Ex 37

Ex 38

14

Ex 39

Ex 40

Ex 41

Ex 42

Ex 43

Ex 44

Reactions with Aldehydes and Ketones

Organocuprates react with aldehydes to give alcohols in high yield. In the presence of chlorotrimethylsilane, the corresponding siliylenol ethers can be obtained.

Ex 45

Ex 46

How will you Synthesis this:-

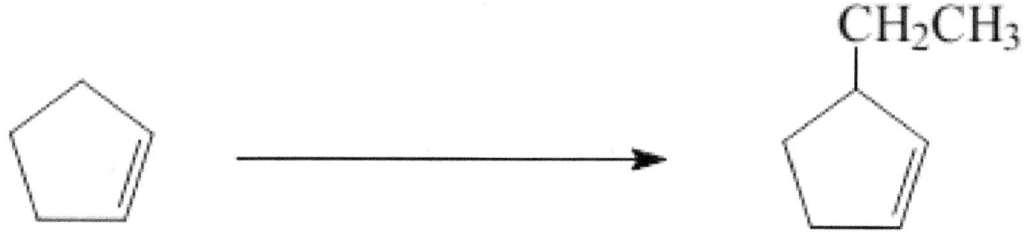

Solution

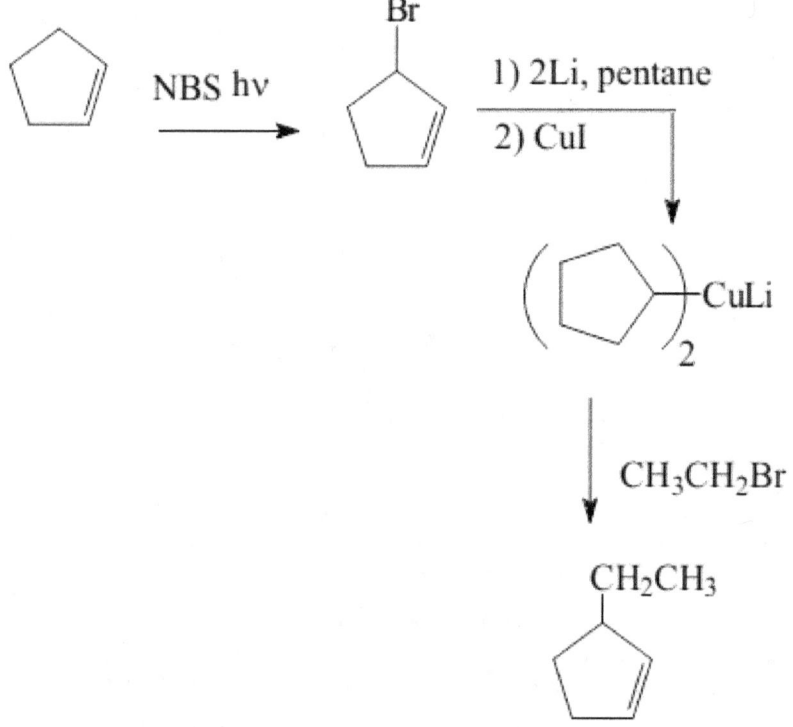

18

Reviews of Lithium Dialkylcopper (organocuprate) $[(R)_2Cu]^-$ Li^+

• Cuprates are less reactive than organolithium

• R acts as a Nucleophile

• Oxidation state of copper is Cu(I).

• Nucleophile "R" will attack various organic electrophiles.

• Organocuprates are used in cross-coupling reactions to form higher alkanes

Cross-Coupling Reaction: coupling of two different alkylsR and R' to yield a

new alkane (R-R'). This type of reaction is used to make new C-C between alkyl

groups.

Limitations

• Methyl and 1° R-X iodides work well

– elimination occurs with 2° and 3 ° R-X

– seems to follow SN_2 conditions

• also works for vinyl and aryl halides

LDA (LITHIUM DIISOPROPYLAMIDE)

LDA(LITHIUM DIISOPROPYLAMIDE)

It can be used to drive the ketone-enolate equilibrium completely to the enolate side. LDA is a strong base that is useful for this purpose. The steric bulk of its isopropyl groups makes LDA nonnucleophilic. Even so, it's a strong base.

Thermodynamic vs. Kinetic Control of Enolate Formation

A
99%

B
1%

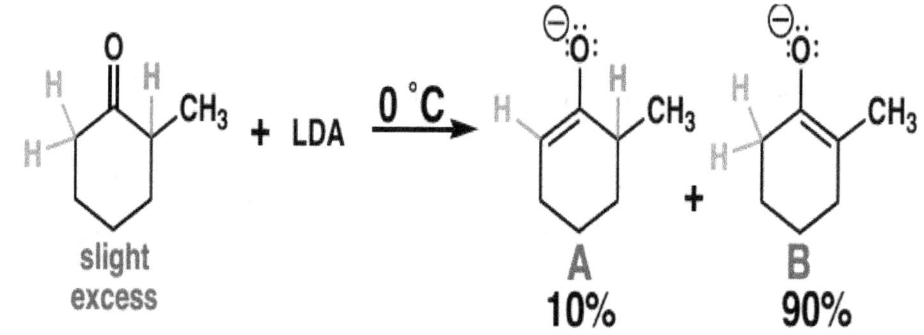
H
H
H
O
CH3
+ LDA
0 °C
slight
excess
A
10%
B
90%

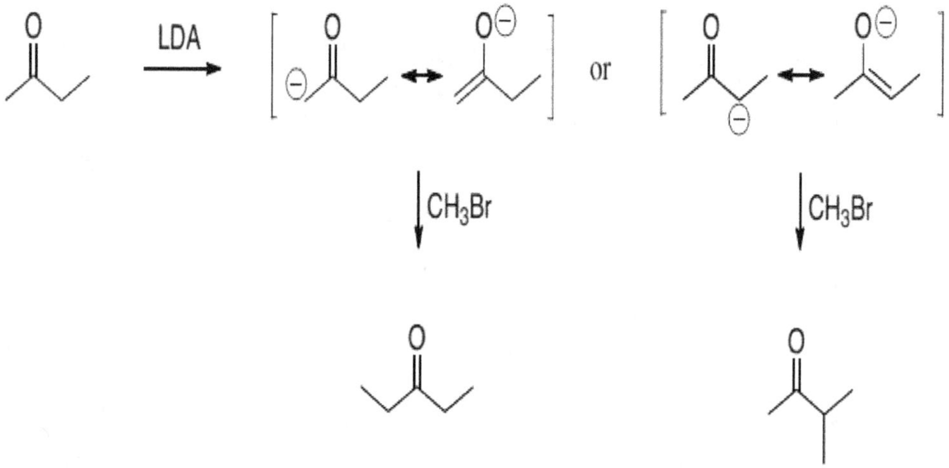
LDA
or
CH3Br
CH3Br

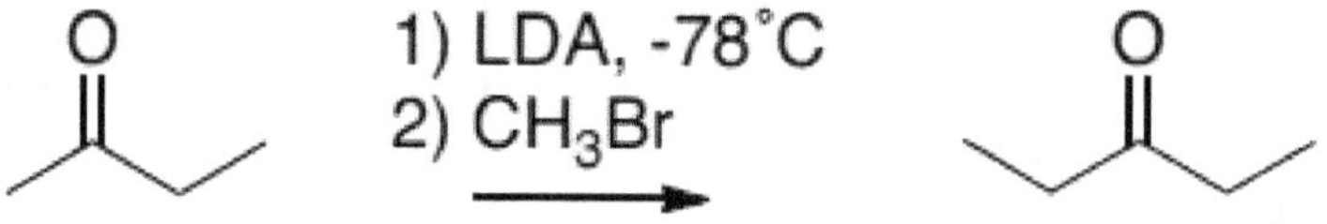
1) LDA, -78°C
2) CH3Br

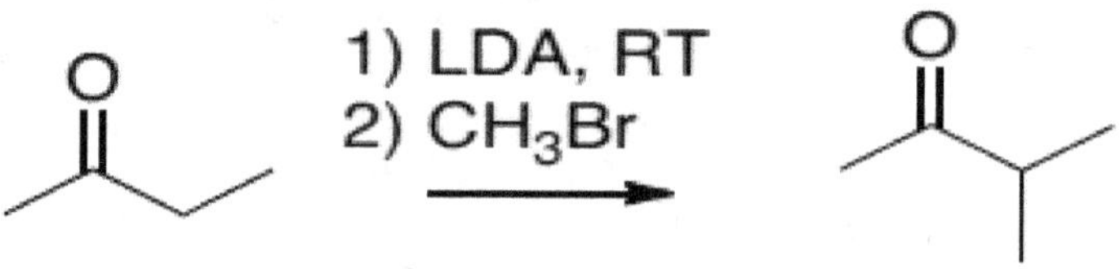
1) LDA, RT
2) CH3Br

LDA is a strong base (pKa of conjugate is close to 40), while it is very bulky so it will not react as nucleophile on carbonyl. The most common use of LDA is in the formation of enolates. LDA will remove the proton selectively from the carbon substituted with the fewest number of carbons.

Formation of enolates

Alkylation of enolates

Halogenation of enolates

Aldol Reaction

Formation of Hoffmann elimination products

Hoffmann Product   **Zaitsev Product**
(major)   (minor)

With an unsymmetrical carbonyl can obtain two different enolates.

Thermodynamic vs. Kinetic Control

The key is the stability of each enolate generated. The enolate can be preferentially

generated at either site depending upon conditions.

Kinetic enolate
easier hydrogen to abstract

Thermodynamic enolate
more stable double bond

Lower temperature favors kinetic product Higher temperatures (in this case usually

room temperature and above)favors thermodynamic product.

25

1) LDA, -78°C
2) CH₃Br

1) LDA, RT
2) CH₃Br

α-alkylation of an aldehyde

To alkylate an aldehyde, first need to convert the aldehyde to a less reactive system.

An imine or imine derivative is used most frequently

—NH₂

LDA

1) CH₃Br
2) H+, H₂O

One product

1. LiN(i-Pr)$_2$, THF
2. butanal
3. H$_3$O$^+$

1) LDA

2)

Convert following

Method 1:

Method 2

Method 3

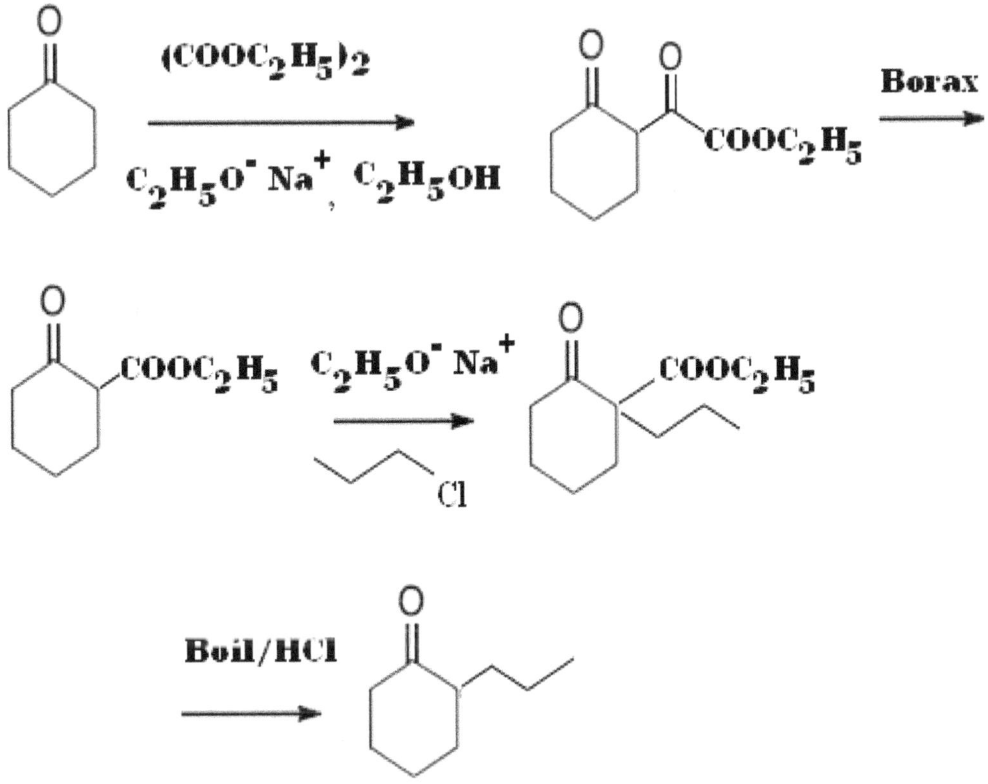
(COOC2H5)2
C2H5O- Na+, C2H5OH
COOC2H5
Borax
COOC2H5
C2H5O- Na+
Cl
COOC2H5
Boil/HCl

N,N'-DICYCLOHEXYLCARBODIIMIDE

$$N=C=N$$

N,N'-DICYCLOHEXYLCARBODIIMIDE

This is an organic compound with the chemical formula $C_{13}H_{22}N_2$ whose primary use is to couple amino acids during artificialpeptide synthesis.

The C-N=C=N-C core of carbodiimides (N=C=N) is linear, being related to the structure of allene.

Three principal resonance structures describe carbodiimides:

$$RN=C=NR \leftrightarrow RN^+\equiv C\text{-}N^-R \leftrightarrow RN^-\text{-}C\equiv N^+R$$

The N=C=N moiety gives characteristic IR spectroscopic signature at $2117\ cm^{-1}$. The ^{15}N NMR spectrum shows a characteristic shift of 275.0 ppm upfield of nitric acid and the ^{13}C NMR spectrum features a peak at about 139 ppm downfield from TMS.

Applications

DCC is a dehydrating agent for the preparation of amides, ketones, nitriles.

In these reactions, DCC hydrates to formdicyclohexylurea (DCU), a compound that is insoluble in most organic solvents and in water and hence is readily removed by filtration. DCC can also be used to invert secondary alcohols.

A solution of DCC and dimethyl sulfoxide (DMSO) effects the so-called Pfitzner-Moffatt oxidation. This procedure is used for the oxidation of alcohols to aldehydes and ketones

The Pfitzner –Moffatt oxidation, sometimes referred to as simply the Moffatt oxidation, is a chemical reaction which describes the oxidation of primary and secondary alcohols by dimethyl sulfoxide (DMSO) activated with a carbodiimide, such as dicyclohexylcarbodiimide (DCC). The resulting alkoxysulfonium ylide rearranges to generate aldehydes and ketones, respectively.

$$RCHOHCH_2R' + (C_6H_{11}N)_2C \rightarrow RCH=CHR' + (C_6H_{11}NH)_2CO$$

Synthesis of Peptides

DCC is useful for the coupling of amino acids *via* amide C-N bonds.

1

2

$$Ph.OH + HO.C_2H_5 \xrightarrow{DCC} Ph.O.C_2H_5 + DCC-H_2O$$

$$RCOOH + HOR' \xrightarrow{DCC} RCOOR' + DCC-H_2O$$

$$RNH_2 + R'COOH \xrightarrow[DCC]{0°} RNHCOR' + DCC-H_2O$$

$$n \text{ Nucleotides} \xrightarrow{DCC} \underset{RNA}{(Nucleotides)_n} + DCC—H_2O$$

$$2R.COOH + C_6H_{11}N=C=N.C_6H_{11} \longrightarrow (RCO)_2O + DCC-H_2O$$

$$2R.SO_3H + C_6H_{11}N=C=N.C_6H_{11} \longrightarrow (RSO_2)_2O + DCC-H_2O$$

For making lactonisation of hydroxyl acids

33

DITHIANE

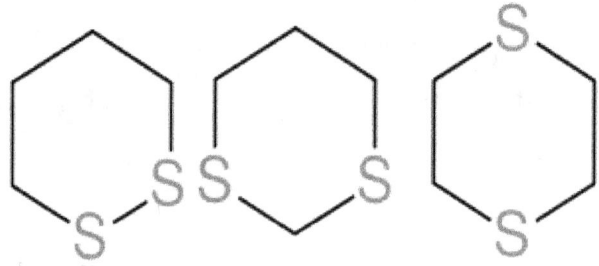

DITHIANE

A dithiane is a heterocyclic compound composed of a cyclohexane core structure wherein two methylene bridges (-CH₂- units) are replaced by sulfurcentres. The three isomeric parent heterocycles are 1,2-dithiane, 1,3-dithiane and 1,4-dithiane.

1,3-Dithianes are protecting group of some carbonyl-containing compounds due to their inertness to many conditions. They form by treatment of the carbonyl compound with 1,3-propanedithiol under conditions that remove water from the system.[1] The protecting group can be removed with mercuric reagents, a process that exploits the high affinity of Hg(II) for thiolates. 1,3-Dithianes are also employed in umpolung reactions, such as the Corey-Seebach reaction

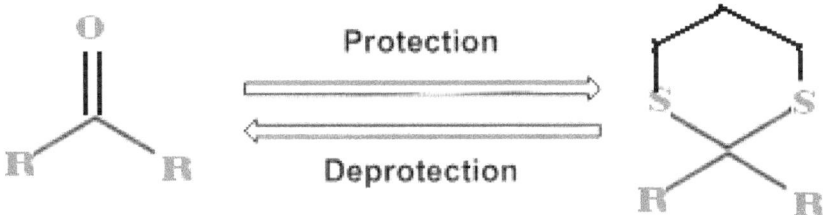

Dithiane has relatively acidic hydrogens located between the two sulfur atoms, and these can be removed by a strong base.

The anion is stabilized by the electron withdrawing effect of the highly polarizable sulfur atoms.

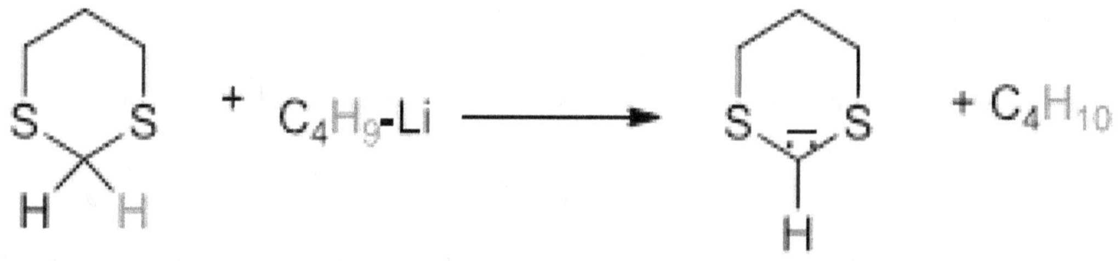
+ C4H9-Li
+ C4H10

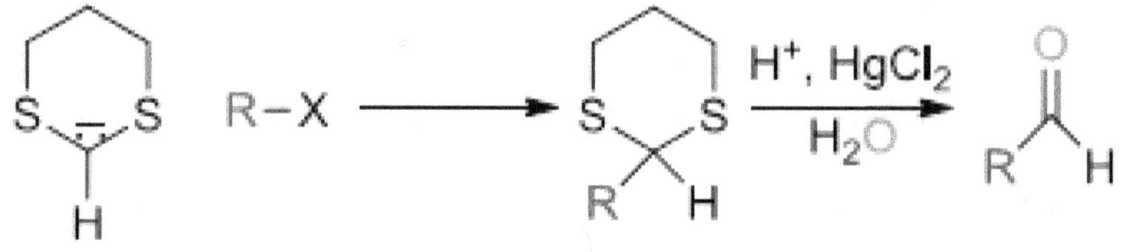
R−X
H+, HgCl2
H2O

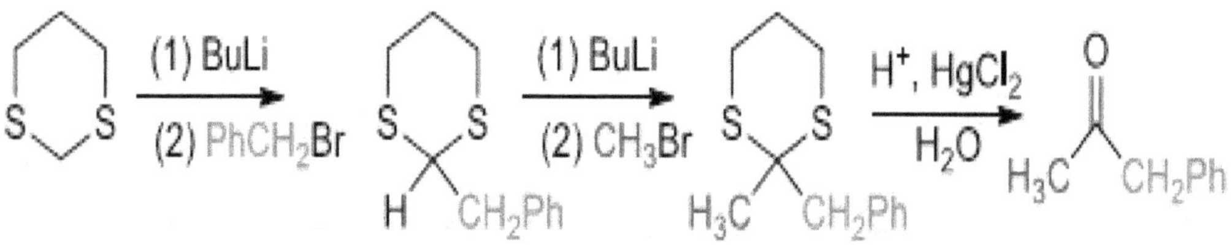
(1) BuLi
(2) PhCH2Br
(1) BuLi
(2) CH3Br
H+, HgCl2
H2O

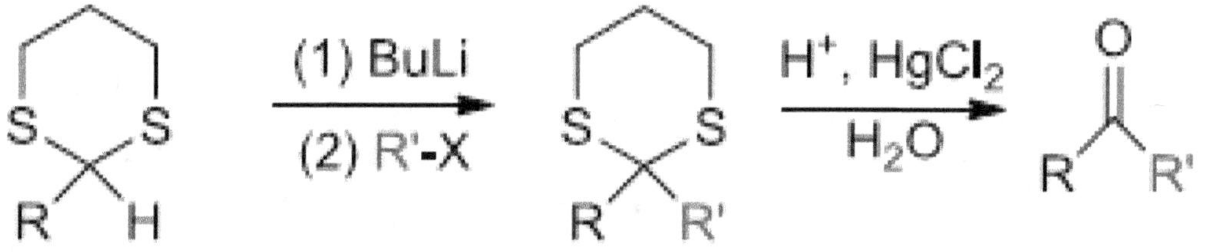
(1) BuLi
(2) R'-X
H+, HgCl2
H2O

The dithiane can be thought of as a "masked" carbonyl group.

SH SH

CHCl$_3$

HCl (g)

THF, - 40°C

Br

OH

OH

OH

OH

OH

S   S   H   S   S   Li

H   H

C$_4$H$_9$Li   R$_2$C=O

1,3-dithiane   2-lithio-1,3-
dithiane

S   C(OH)R$_2$

H   R$_2$C(OH)CH=O

HgO, H$^+$ carbonyl
compound

38

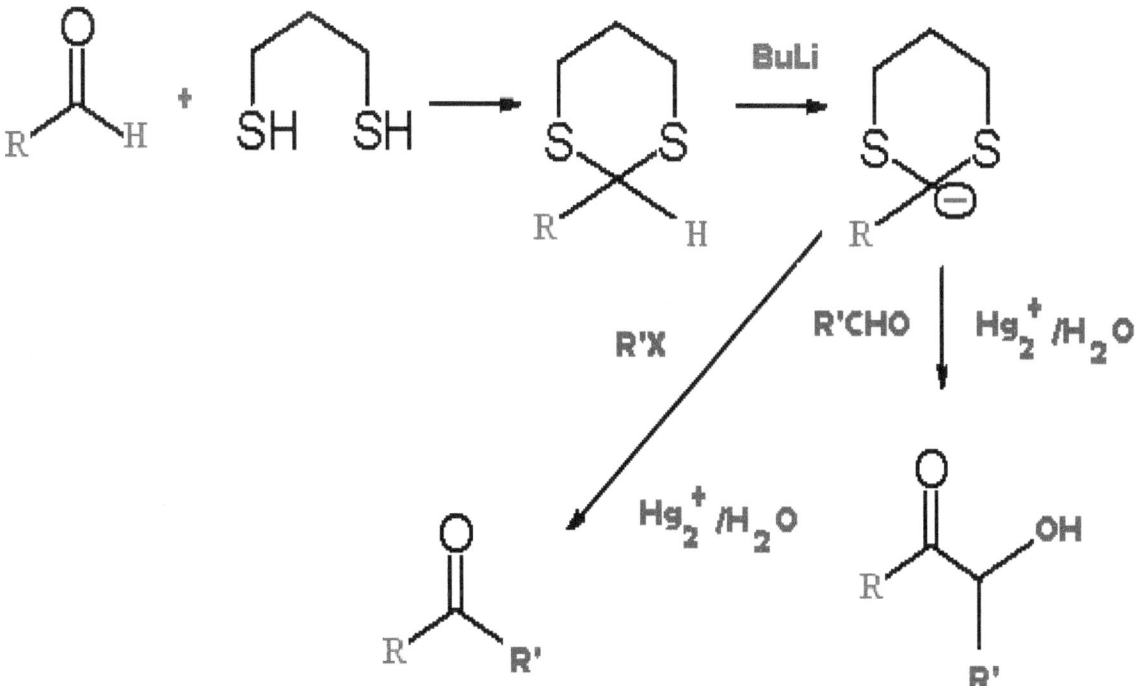

In Short above reaction can be written as

1 HS $(CH_2)_3$ SH
2 BuLi
3 R'X
4 Hg_2^+ / H_2O

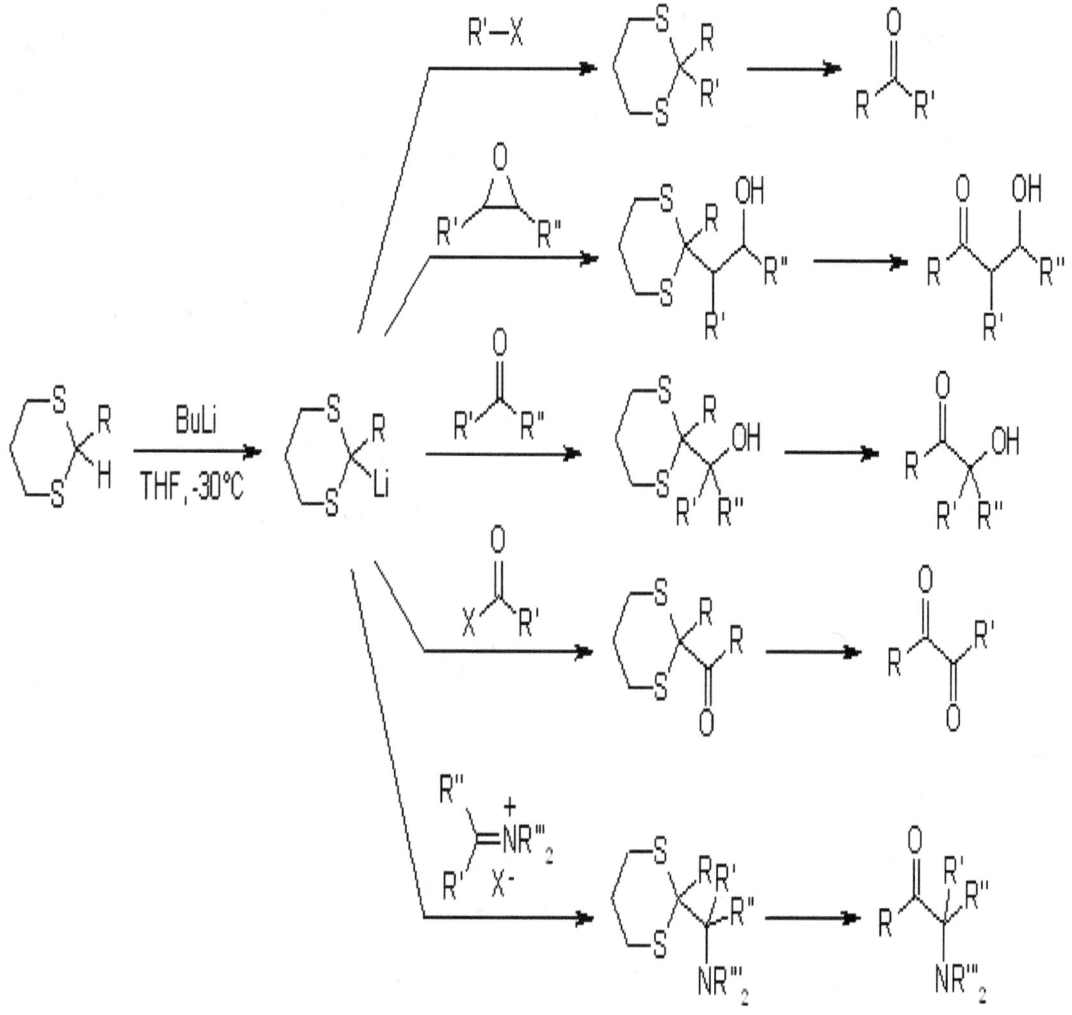

BuLi
THF, -30°C
R'—X

TRIMETHYLSILYL IODIDE

TRIMETHYLSILYL IODIDE

Iodotrimethylsilane, $(CH_3)_3SiI$, or Trimethylsilyl iodide, is an organosilicon compound. It is a colorless, volatile liquid at room temperature.

Trimethylsilyl iodide is used to introduce the trimethylsilyl group onto alcohols(ROH):

ROH + TMSI → RO(TMS) + HI

This type of reaction may be useful for gas chromatography analysis.

Nu = H_2N, MeNH, SPh

TRIBUTYLTIN HYDRIDE

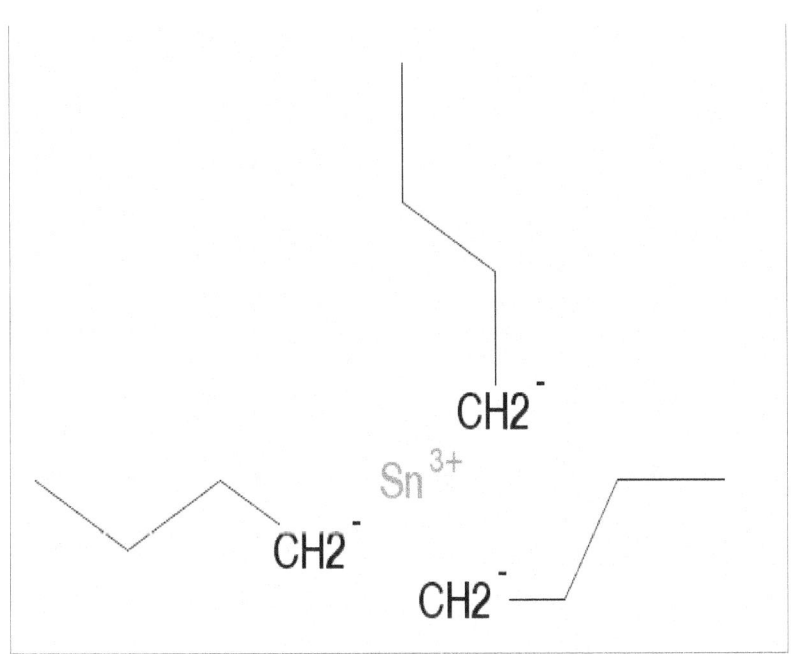

TRIBUTYLTIN HYDRIDE

Tributyltin hydride is an organotin compound with the formula $(C_4H_9)_3SnH$. It is a colorless liquid that is soluble in organic solvents. The compound is used as a source of hydrogen atoms in organic synthesis.

It substitute halogen atom of alkyl halide with –H atom.

$$R\,X \longrightarrow R\,H$$

Low concentration of Tributyltin hydride leads to cyclization reaction and in case of bulky groups are present no cyclization reaction happens. It is a useful reagent in organic synthesis. Combined with azobisisobutyronitrile(AIBN) or by irradiation with light, tributyltin hydride converts organic halides (and related groups) to the corresponding hydrocarbon.

Ex 1

Ex 2

Ex 3

Ex 4

Ex 5

Ex 6

Ex 7

Ex 8

Ex 9

Ex 10

Bu$_3$Sn-H, AIBN

Ex 11

RCOCl

NaO–N

t-BuSH

hν or Δ

R–H

Barton ester

Ex 12

(Major)

Ex 13

Ex 14

Ex 15

Ex 16

Ex 17

Ex 18

Ex 19

RX + H$_2$C=CHCN $\xrightarrow{\text{(H}_3\text{C)}_3\text{C–SnH}}$ RCH$_2$CH$_2$CN

Mechanism

(H$_3$C)$_3$C–SnH $\longrightarrow$ (H$_3$C)$_3$C–Sn·

(H$_3$C)$_3$C–Sn· + RX $\longrightarrow$ R· + (H$_3$C)$_3$C–SnX

R· + H$_2$C=CHCN $\longrightarrow$ RCH$_2$ĊHCN

RCH$_2$ĊHCN + (H$_3$C)$_3$C–SnH $\longrightarrow$ RCH$_2$CH$_2$CN + (H$_3$C)$_3$C–Sn·

Ex 20

$\xrightarrow[\text{AIBN, nBu}_3\text{SnH}]{\text{(MeO)}_3\text{P}}$

Ex 21

Ex 22

Ex 23

Ex 24

i) NaH, CS$_2$
ii) MeI

iii) Bu$_3$SnH, AIBN

Ex 25

INTERMOLECULAR ADDITION REACTIONS

- TBT generates synthetically useful radicals

- addition reactions

C-I good as weak

electron deficient alkene so
radical *nucleophilic*

$$\text{TBTH, AIBN,} \atop \text{Heat}$$

C-Cl normally too
strong

electron-rich alkene

$$\text{TBTH, AIBN,} \atop \text{Heat}$$

EWG stabilise radical so readily
formed. Make radical electron deficient
so *electrophilic*

Ex 26

Ex 27

Intra-molecular addition: radical based ring-formation reactions

- if a radical is joined to a double bond by a chain of three or more carbons intramolecular addition generates a ring.

- radical reactions readily form 5 membered rings

- formation of 5-ring takes place under *kinetic* control (energy of transition state for the formation of 5-ring lower than that for 6-ring)

Vinyl radicals

Ex 28

Ex 29

Ex 30

58

Ex 31

R $\overset{S}{\underset{}{\|}}$ O

C_6H_5OCO

C_6H_5OCO

$OCOC_6H_5$

O O

H_3C CH_3

$\xrightarrow[\text{AIBN, } C_6H_6]{(C_4H_9)_3SnH}$

C_6H_5OCO

CH_3

H_3C

O

O

H_3C

$OCOC_6H_5$

Ex 32

CH_2

$C_6H_5SO_2-N$

CH_3

Br

$\xrightarrow[\text{AIBN, } C_6H_6]{(C_4H_9)_3SnH}$

CH_3

$C_6H_5SO_2-N$

CH_3

Ex 33

Br

$\xrightarrow[\text{AIBN, } C_6H_6]{(C_4H_9)_3SnH}$

$CH_2\cdot$

$CH_2\cdot$

or

$CH\cdot$

$-CH_2\cdot$ $\longrightarrow$ 85%

CH_3

+

$\longrightarrow$ 5% CH_2

10%

CH_3

Ex 34

Ex 35

Ex 36

Ex 37

Ex 38

Ex 39

Ex 39

Ex 40

Ex 41

62

Ex 42

Ex 43

Ex 44

Ex 45

Ex 46

Ex 47

64

Ex 48

Ex 49

Ex 50

Ex 51

Ex 52

Ex 53

Ex 54

SULFIDES AND SELENIDES

Ex 55

Ex 56

ALCOHOL DERIVATIVES

- Deoxygenation of alcohols a good method for preparing carbon-centred radicals

- Good for primary and secondary alcohols but not for tertiary (3° radicals less stable)

driving force is
- strrength of
C=O bond

MULTIPLE BONDS

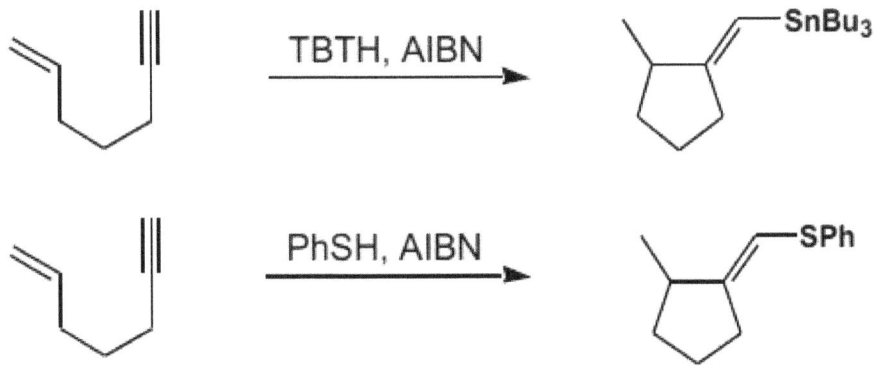

GROUP OR ATOM TRANSFER: HALOGEN

Mechanism

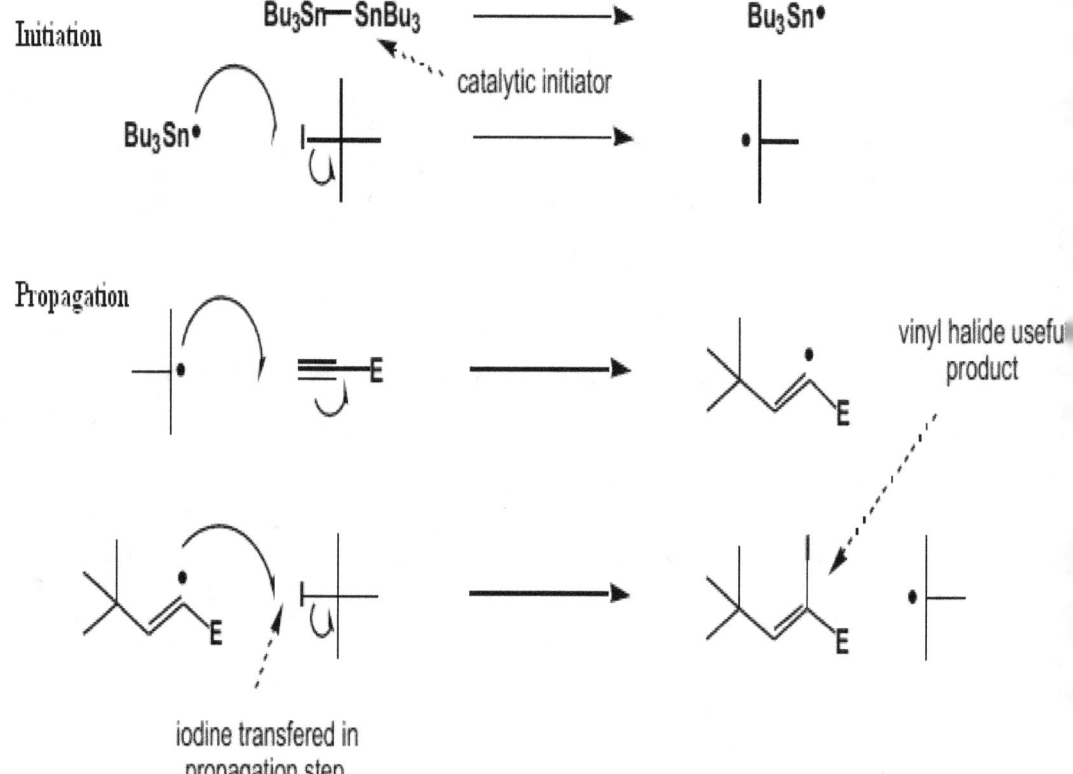

Initiation

Bu₃Sn—SnBu₃ ⟶ Bu₃Sn•

catalytic initiator

Bu₃Sn•

Propagation

vinyl halide useful product

iodine transfered in propagation step

TANDEM CYCLISATIONS

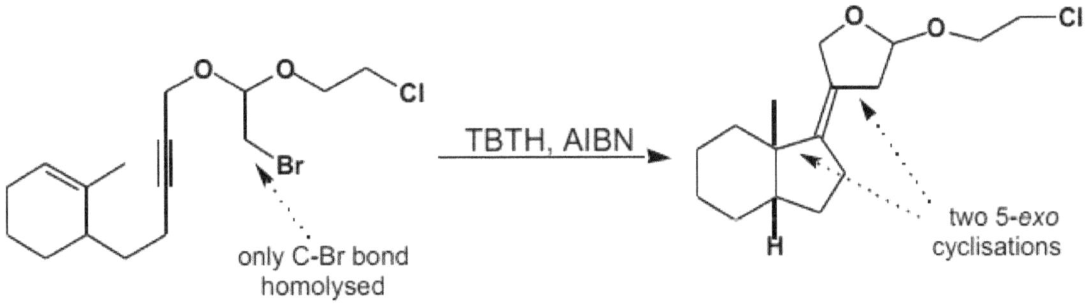

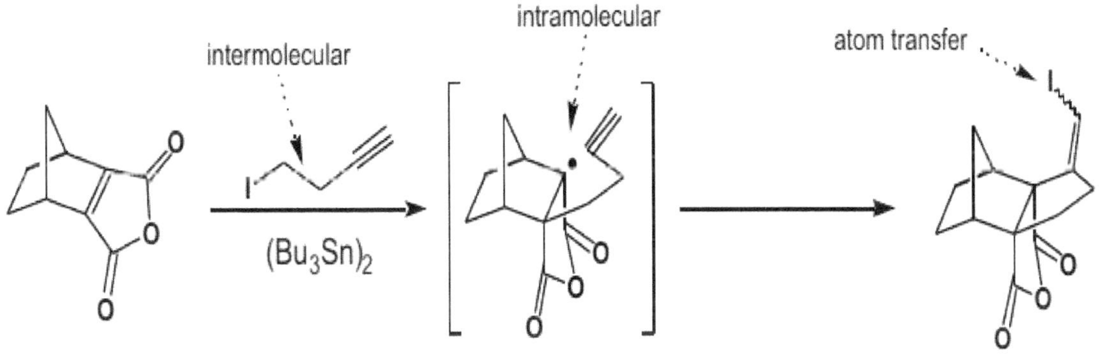

only C-Br bond homolysed

TBTH, AIBN

two 5-*exo* cyclisations

intermolecular

intramolecular

atom transfer

$(Bu_3Sn)_2$

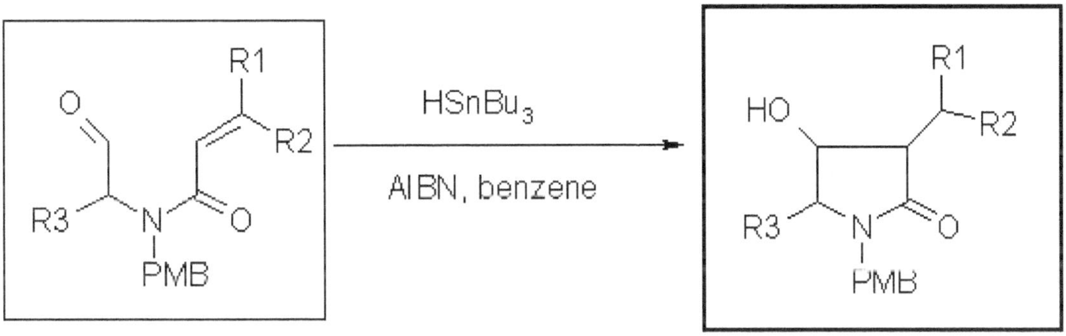

R1

R2

R3

N

PMB

$HSnBu_3$

AIBN, benzene

HO

R1

R2

R3

N

PMB

Barton-Mccombie Deoxygenation

GIVE MECHANISM FOR THE GIVEN REACTION

Solution

WOODWARD PREVOST HYDROXYLATION

WOODWARD REACTION

Woodward *cis*-Hydroxylation

The Woodward Reaction allows the synthesis of *syn*-diols from alkenes by the addition of iodine followed by nucleophilic displacement with acetate in the presence of water. Hydrolysis of the intermediate ester gives the desired diol.

The Prévost Reaction gives *anti*-diols

Mechanism

initial addition of iodine leads to a cyclic iodonium ion, that is opened through nucleophilic substitution by acetate anion:

A cyclic acetoxonium ion is then formed:

In contrast to the course of the Prévost Reaction, water appears to add readily as a nucleophile to the partially positive carbon atom of the intermediate. The cyclic orthoacetate is then cleaved to a monoacylated diol:

The desired diol can be isolated after hydrolysis.

76

PRÉVOST REACTION

OSMIUM TETROXIDE

OSMIUM TETROXIDE

The osmium of OsO₄ has an oxidation number of VIII, however the metal does not possess a corresponding 8+ charge as the bonding in the compound is largely covalent in character (the ionization energy required to produce a formal 8+ charge also far exceeds the energies available in normal chemical reactions).

The osmium atom has eight valence electrons ($6s^2$, $5d^6$) with double bonds to the four oxide ligands resulting in a 16 electron complex.

This is isoelectronic with permanganate and chromateions.

Oxidation of alkenes

Alkenes add to OsO₄ to give diolate species that hydrolyze to cis-diols.

OsO₄ is a Lewis acid and a mild oxidant. Most of its reactions reflect this pattern. It reacts with alkaline aqueous solution to give the perosmate anion $OsO_4(OH)_2^{2-}$.[14] This species is easily reduced to osmate anion, $OsO_2(OH)_4^{4-}$.

Organic synthesis

In organic synthesis OsO_4 is widely used to oxidise alkenes to the vicinal diols, adding two hydroxyl groups at the same side (syn addition).

Cis   Meso

Trans   Racemic Mixture

DICHLORO DICYANO QUINONE (DDQ)

2,3-Dichloro-5,6-dicyano-1,4-benzoquinone

DICHLORO DICYANO QUINONE (DDQ)

DDQ is a member of large family of benzoquinones.

DDQ can be used as an oxidant and a dehydrogenation agent.

During the reaction 2,3-Dichloro-5,6-dicyanohydroquinone (=DDQH) is formed

Applications

1.Dehydrogenation of hydrocarbons

Chromenes

Dehydrogenation of Carbonyl Compounds

DDQ is a versatile reagent for the synthesis of α,β-unsaturated carbonyl compounds.

2. Aromatization

Aromatization of steroids may occur with a Wagner-Meerwein rearrangement3.
It allows to dehydrogenate systems containing quaternary atoms without loss of
carbon.

3. Dehydrogenation of carbonyl compounds and steroids

DDQ is a versatile reagent in the synthesis of a,b-unsaturated compounds, such as 3-keto-steroïds4. Regioselective dehydrogenation of 3-keto-steroïds depends on the geometry of the molecule at the C-5 atom. The selectivity of one isomer is likely to reflect the relative steric crowding of the C-4 hydrogen atom for the two series.

5-α−

5-β−

4. Dehydrogenation of carbonyl compounds

DDQ, BSTFA

DDQ, HCl or chloranil

DDQ

6. Oxidation of Alcohol

DDQ, Acetone

88

7. Oxidation of Phenol and cyclization

Intermolecular coupling may occur if phenols and enolizable ketones cannot undergo a,b-dehydrogenation.

Phenolic compounds treated with DDQ can be used to make oxygen containing heterocycles i.e. coumarins, chromenes and benzofurans.

DDQ can be used to make C-C or C-O couplings

8. Allylic and benzylic ethers

The conversion of allylic and benzylic ethers to corresponding carbonyl compounds.

In dry conditions DDQ can be used for intramolecular oxidative formation.

in aqueous conditions the dimethoxybenzyl group is cleaved

Aryl-propene double bond can be oxidized in several products

9. Oxidative De-protection

DDQ has been described as a powerful and selective reagent in the deprotection reactions, in several articles and patents.

10. DDQ has also been used as a mediator in carbon-carbon bond formation, or as a cyanation agent.

Ex.1

Ex.2

Ex.3

Ex.4

Ex.5

DDQ

Ex.6

DDQ

Ex.7

DDQ

95

Ex.8

Ex.9

DDQ

toluene
116°C, 8h

96%

Ex.10

O_2

DDQ/NaNO$_2$

Ex.11

+ DDQ

conditions

SELENIUM DOXIDE

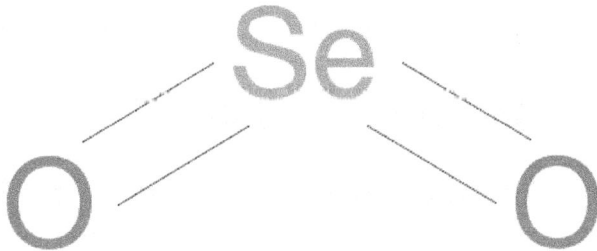

Importance:

1. To oxidize allylic and benzylic –CH to corresponding –OH group

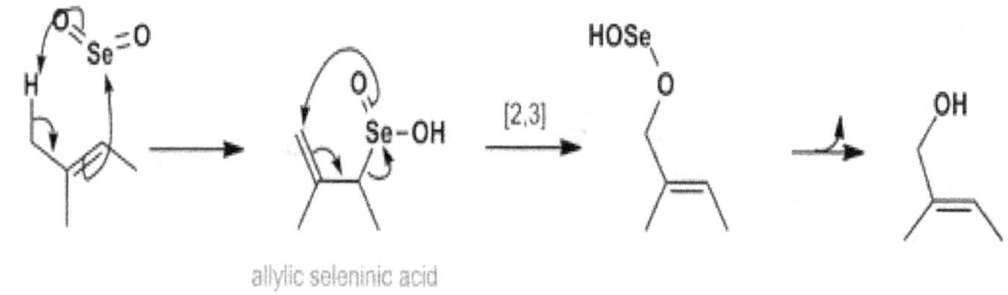

allylic seleninic acid

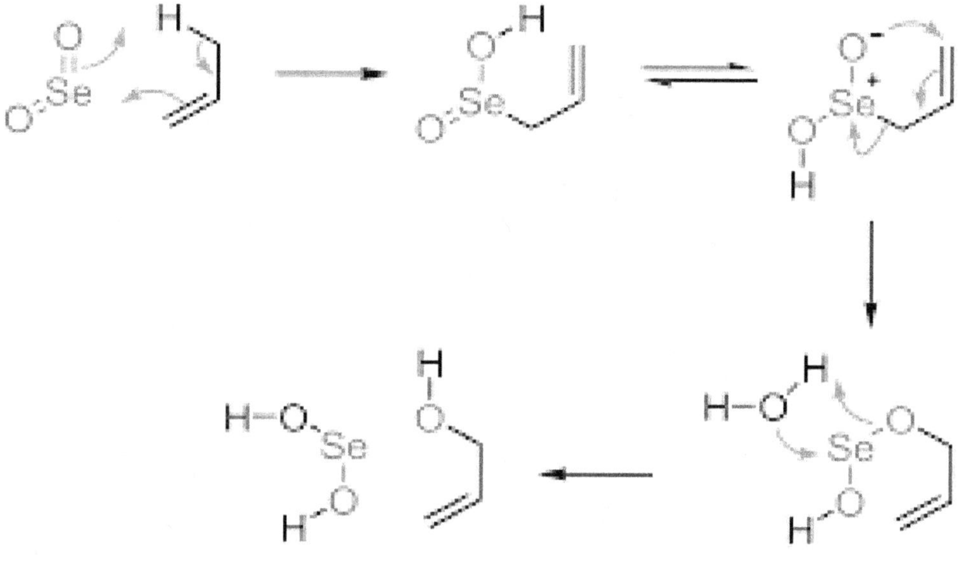

2. To oxidize –CH$_2$ to –CO- group

Eg CH3CHO→ CHO-CHO, C2H5COCH3→C2H5COCHO

Dehydrogenation and hydroxylation

3. SeO_2 will convert an allylic methylene group into the corresponding alcohol.

4. oxidize the α-methylene group adjacent to a carbonyl group to give a 1,2-dicarbonyl compound

5. Selenium oxide can also be used to oxidize alkynes in presence of acids. The internal alkynes are converted to 1,2-dicarbonyl compounds, whereas terminal alkynes are oxidized to glyoxylic acids

It also oxidizes benzylic methylene, CH_2 group to C=O

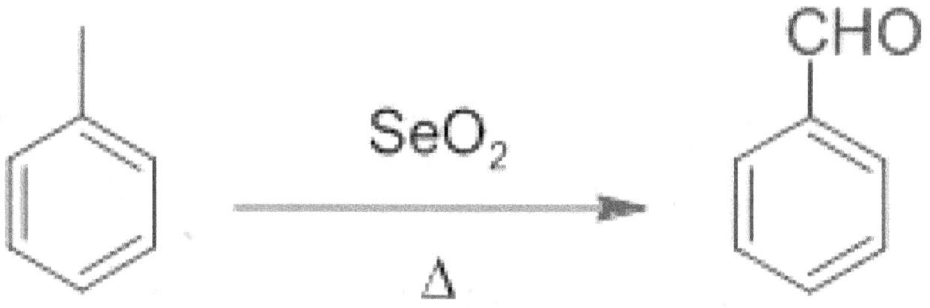

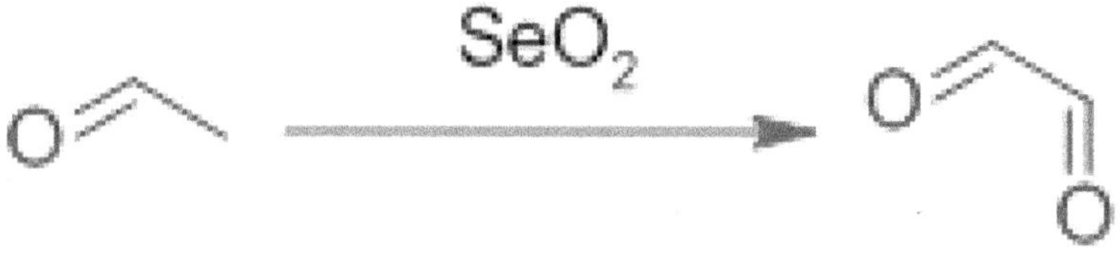

SeO₂
Δ

oxidation to 1,2-dicarbonyl compound

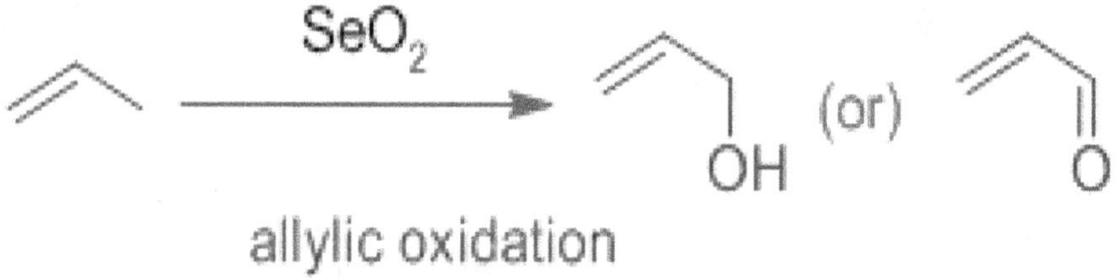

SeO₂

allylic oxidation

Ex 1

SeO₂

Ex 2

Ex 3

Ex 4

Ex 5

Ex 6

Ex 7

Ex 8

Ex 9

Ex 10

Ex 11

Ex 12

Ex 13

Ex 14

Ex 15

Ex 16

Ex 17

Hamigeran B

Ex 18

Ex 19

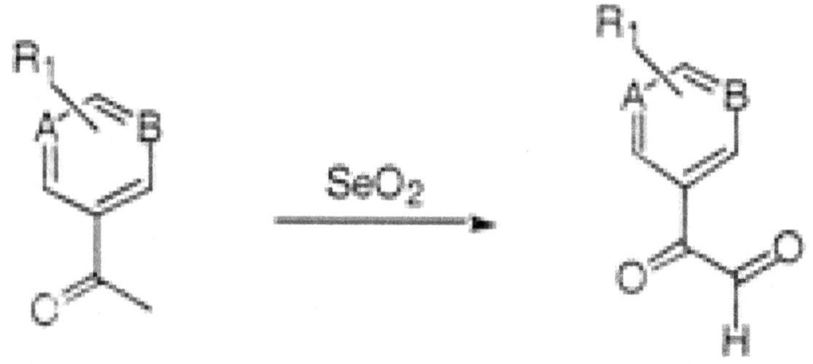

Ex 20

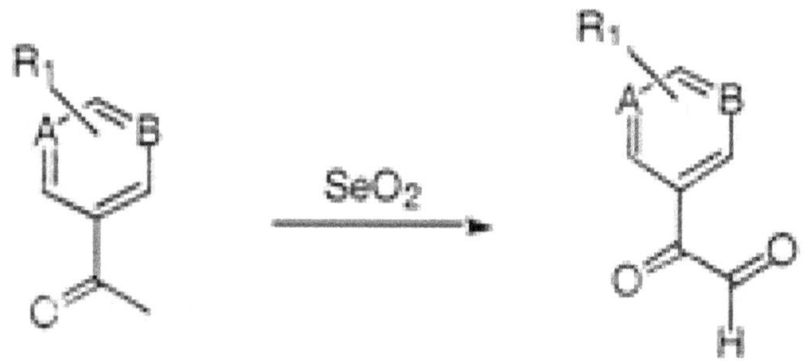

Ex 21

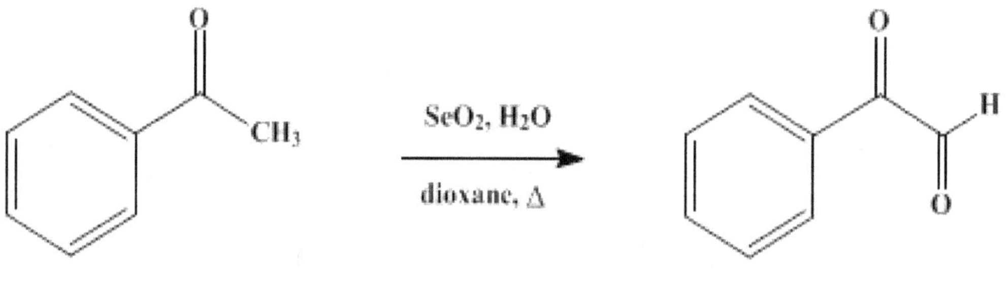

Catalytic amount of selenium dioxide and t-BuOOH can be employed in the allylic oxidation of cyclohexene to cyclohex-2-en-1-ol, an allylic alcohol. A catalytic amount of SeO₂ along with an oxidizing agent like t-butyl hydroperoxide, that reoxidizes the selenium(II) compounds after each cycle of the reaction.

Ex 22

Ex 23

(-) - β - pinene   (+) - *trans* - pinocarveol

Trisubstituted alkenes are oxidized selectively at more substituted end of double bond by giving E-allylic alcohols or conjugated carbonyl compounds

The allylic oxidation occurs predominantly at most nucleophilic double bond

Oxidation takes place at alpha position to the more substituted end of the double bond.

It oxidize methyl group adjacent to unsaturated group such as -CO, C=C, -CN to –CHO and –CH2 to –CO- group

PHASE-TRANSFER CATALYST

A phase transfer catalyst is a catalyst which facilitates the migration of a reactant in a heterogeneous system from one phase into another phase where reaction can take place. Ionic reactants are often soluble in an aqueous phase but are insoluble in an organic phase unless the phase transfer catalyst is present

PRINCIPLE OF PHASE-TRANSFER CATALYSIS

The principle of PTC is based on the ability of certain íphase-transfer agents (the PT catalysts) to facilitate the transport of one reagent from one phase into another (immiscible) phase wherein the other reagent exists. Thus, reaction is made possible by bringing together the reagents which are originally in different phases. However, it is also necessary that the transferred species is in an active state for effective PT catalytic action, and that it is regenerated during the organic reaction.

The simplest examples of these processes are generally biphasic phase-transfer reactions in which the catalyst facilitates reaction by solublizing a reagent or substrate ion in the organic phase.

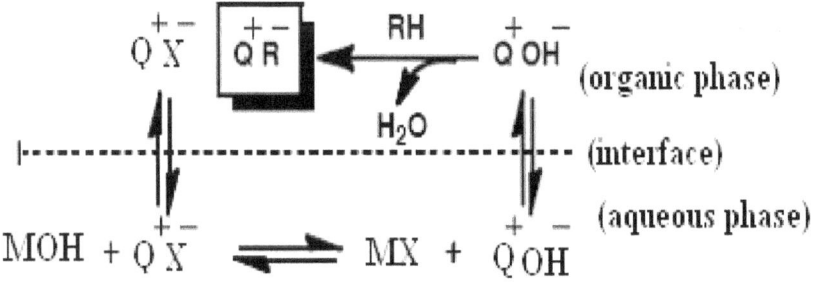

Starks Extraction Mechanism of Phase-Transfer Catalysis

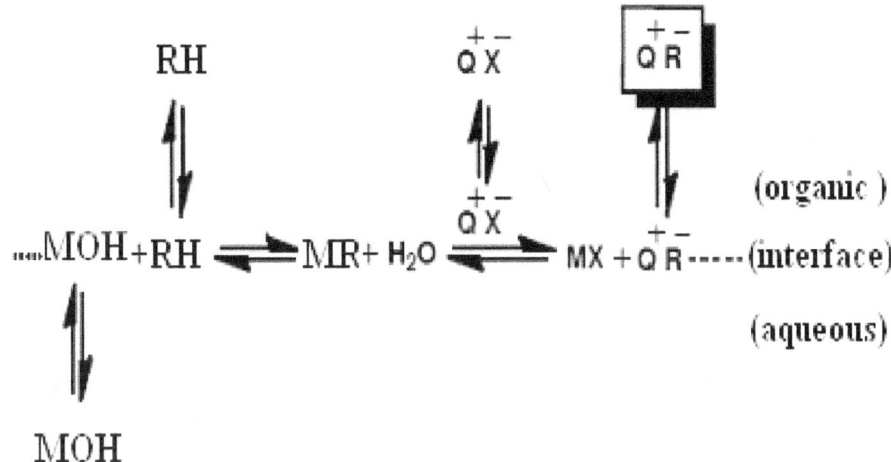

Makosza Interfacial Mechanism of Phase-Transfer Catalysis

In Starks's mechanism the PTC (Q+X-) exchange ion with base at the water phase to give Q+OH-, then it will go into the organic phase and deprotonate the substrate to give Q+R-. The ion pair (Q+R-) will carry on doing other reactions.

In Makosza's mechanism, the deprotonation happened at the interface between the base and substrate. The resulting ion pair (M+R-) exchange ion with PTC (Q+X-) to give the Q+R- and carry on doing further reactions.

111

PT catalysts

Agents used as PT catalysts are onium salts (ammonium and phosphonium salts), macrocyclic polyethers (crown ethers), aza-macrobicyclic ethers (cryptands), open chain polyethers (polyethylene glycols, PEGS, and their dimethyl ethers, glymes).

Quatemary onium salts (commonly called as quats) are the most widely used PT catalysts, with ammonium and phosphonium salts being industrially most feasible. A quaternary ammonium salt can also be generated in situ in cases where tertiary amines are used as PT agents.

Macrocyclic and macrobicyclic polydentate ligands like crown ethers and cryptands are widely used as PT catalysts, especially in solid-liquid systems, due to their ability to complex and solubilize metal cations, along with the corresponding anion to maintain charge balance, However, despite their high activity as effective PT catalysts, crown ethers and cryptands are not feasible for most industrial applications due their high costs and toxicity. Open chain polyethers like polyethylene glycols (PEGS) and their many derivatives are also widely used as PT catalysts. Although less active than quaternary ammonium salts and crown ethers, they are relatively less costly and environmentally safe. PEGS are stable, easy to recover, nontoxic and easily biodegradable, and are easily available. For reactions involving hydroxide transfer in solid-liquid systems in moderately polar organic solvents, PEGS are very good PT catalysts with activities sometimes better than those of crown ethers. Solubility in water makes them poor catalysts for liquid-liquid systems, although in some cases the PEG may form a third catalyst-rich phase and function as an active PT catalyst.

Various other novel PT catalysts have been developed which find specific applications in certain types of reactions. For example, Kondo et al. (1988, 1989, 1994, and references therein) have been developed polymeric analogs of dipolar aprotic solvents like dimethyl sulfoxide, N-N-dimethylformamide, N-methyl-2-pyrrolidone, tetramethylurea, and so on in both soluble and immobilized forms. Similarly, chiral PT catalysts based on optically activeamines like ephedrine, chinine, or other cinchona alkaloids are widely used (Bhattacharya et al., 1986). TDA-1 (tris(3,6-dioxahelptyl) amine), synthesized by Rhone-Poulenc, is a stable and effective PT catalyst for solid-liquid reactions, stable both under strongly basic conditions, and at high temperatures (Lavelle, 1986). Brunelle (1987) reported the use of a novel high-temperature PT catalyst, EtHexDMAP (N-alkyl salt of 4-dialkylaminopyridine) for polymers and monomer synthesis. Idoux and Gupton (1987) report the use of polymer bound PT catalysts with more than one PTC site on the polymer. Similar multisite PT catalysts can also be synthesized in their solublenonpolymeric forms from simple polyhalo substrates. Balakrishnan and Jayachandran (1995) recently reported the use of a new rnultisite diammonium dichloride as a PT catalyst in the addition of diochloro-carbene to styrene. Shaffer and Kramer (1990) report a special combination of PTC with inverse PTC (Section on PTC in the Industry) for polymerization reactions called bimechanistic PTC where an ammonium salt was used to mediate transfer from the aqueous phase to the organic phase while a cyclic or an acyclic sulfide like tetrahydrothiophene served as an independent catalysts for the organic to aqueous phase transfer.

Application of PT catalyst

- The reactivity of the reagent anion (R-) in the organic phase is usually enhanced since the Q+R- ion pair tends to have greater charge separation and reduced hydration compared to aqueous solutions of the precursor salt (MOH). Consequently intrinsic reaction rates tend to be significantly higher than those obtained in homogeneous media.

- PTC reaction processes are generally more selective (less side reactions) than homogeneous reactions due to controlled delivery of the reagent into the substrate containing phase.

114

- The reaction conditions are usually compatible with a wide variety of (water-immiscible) organic solvents. This allows the opportunity to select a solvent that is optimal for recovery or reuse or both in prior or subsequent synthetic steps. In addition, it is sometimes possible to utilize the substrate itself as the organic phase, thus eliminating the need for any organic solvent.

- The biphasic nature of these processes greatly simplifies reagent and byproduct separation and hence product isolation. This makes PTC reactions highly attractive alternatives to processes that use polar, water-miscible solvents.

- PTC is particularly useful for reactions of organic anions with nonpolar organic reactants.

- PTC is also applicable for numerous reactions in which anions are intermediates for generating otheractive species such as carbenes, nitrenes and organometallic reagents.

- Reactions have been done in the following areas:

  1)Alkylations\

  2) Substitutions

  3) Aldol and related condensations

  4) Carbenes reactions

5) Oxidations and reductions

6) Organometallic transformations

PTC Reactions

Example 1

The displacement reaction of 1-chlorooctane with aqueous sodium cyanide is accelerated many thousand-fold by the addition of hexadecyltributylphosphonium bromide 1 as a phase-transfer catalyst. The key element of this tremendous reactivity enhancement is the generation of quaternary phosphonium cyanide, which renders the cyanide anion organic soluble and sufficiently nucleophilic.

$$C_8H_{17}Cl \xrightarrow[\text{NaCN, H}_2O]{Bu_3\overset{+}{P}(CH_2)_{15}CH_3\,Br^-} C_8H_{17}CN$$

Example 2

Consider the following reaction:

No Reaction

The 1-chlorooctane and sodium cyanide solution form two separate layers.

Heating of this two phase mixture under reflux and vigorous stirring for 1-2 days

gives no reaction.

Near 100% yield in 2-3 h

When an appropriate quaternary ammonium salt is added, tetrahexylammonium

chloride, the discplacement occurs rapidly in near 100% in 2-3h.

In this process the ammonium salt catalyst:

1) Transfers the cyanide into the organic phase.

2) Activates the transferred cyanide for the reaction with the alkyl halide.

3) Transfers the discplaced chloride anions back to the aqueous phase to start a new catalytic cycle

Mechanism

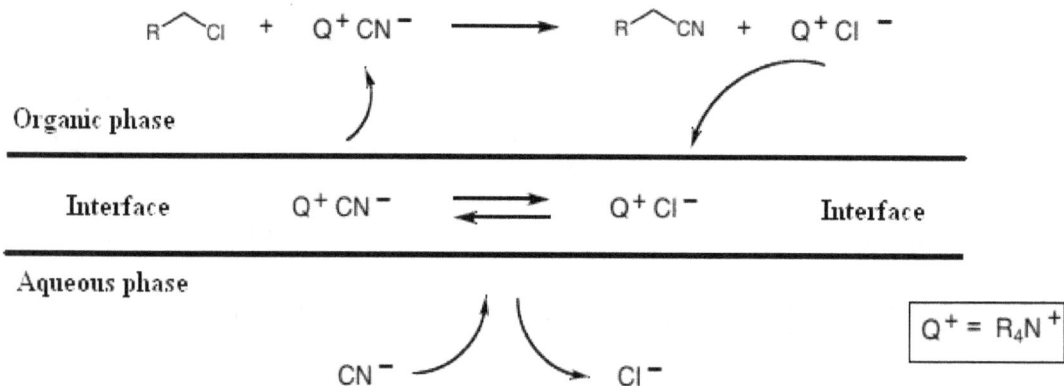

The reaction occurs in at least two steps

Step 1: The intrinsic reaction or organic phase displacement reaction step

   -if this step is rate demining then **EXTRACTION MECHANISM**

Step 2: The transfer step

   -if this step is rate demining then **INTERFACIAL MECHANISM**

Example 3

Alkylations are the most common application of PTC

Example 4

Example 5

Example 6

Reaction with generation of carbine

Under PTC, the carbene is formed in the organic phase, away from the base and the water which minimizes hydrolysis

$$\text{CHCl}_3 \text{ (org)} + \text{Na}^+\text{OH}^- \text{(aq)} \rightleftharpoons \text{Na}^+\text{CCl}_3^- \text{ (int)} + \text{H}_2\text{O (aq)}$$

$$\text{Na}^+\text{CCl}_3^- \text{ (int)} + \text{Q}^+\text{Br}^- \text{ (org)} \rightleftharpoons \text{Q}^+\text{CCl}_3^- \text{ (org)} + \text{Na}^+\text{Cl}^- \text{ (aq)}$$

$$\text{Q}^+\text{CCl}_3^- \text{(org)} \rightleftharpoons \text{CCl}_2 \text{ (org)} + \text{Q}^+\text{Br}^- \text{ (org)}$$

Example 7

Catalyst:

Example 8

Cat.

Example 9

Catalyst:

Example 10

Catalyst:

X = OMe
X = Et

Example 11

Catalyst:

Example 12

$$\text{R}^1 \overset{\text{O}}{\diagdown} \text{R}^2 \quad \xrightarrow[\substack{11\% \text{ NaOCl} \\ \text{PhMe} \\ \text{RT, 4-48hrs}}]{10 \text{ mol\% Cat.}} \quad \text{R}^1 \overset{\text{O}}{\diagdown} \text{R}^2$$

Example 13

Catalyst:

Example 14

Darzens Condensation Reaction

The Darzens Reaction is the condensation of a carbonyl compound with an α-halo ester in the presence of a base to form an α,β-epoxy ester.

Ex1

Cat. (10 mol%)

KOH/toluene

Catalyst:

Ex 2

Cat. (10 mol%)

LiOH·2H$_2$O
BuO$_2$, 4 °C

Catalyst:

Ex 3

Catalyst:

Ex 4

Catalyst:

Ex5

Catalyst:

Ar = 3,5-Ph$_2$C$_6$H$_3$

Ex 6

Catalyst:

Ar = 3,5-Ph$_2$C$_6$H$_3$

CROWN ETHERS & MERRIFIELD RESIN

CROWN ETHER

A crown ether is an ether whose molecule features three or more ether groups in the same ring with any two adjacent ether groups always separated by two carbon atoms. The term "crown" refers to the similarity of the molecular models of the compounds to a regal crown and to the ability of these compounds to "crown" cations by complexation.

The general structural formula of unsubstituted crown ethers is

$$(OCH_2CH_2)_n$$
$$n \geq 3$$

The common name of an unsubstituted crown ether is 3n–crown–n

Nomenclature

Crown ethers are named as x-crown-y where x denotes the total number of atoms in the cyclic backbone and y denotes the number of oxygen/hetero atoms.

[18]-crown-6 has 18 atoms in the ring including the hetero atoms, which is oxygen in this case and has six oxygen atoms, which are the hetero atoms.

If a model of this molecule is made it resembles a crown hence the word "crown".

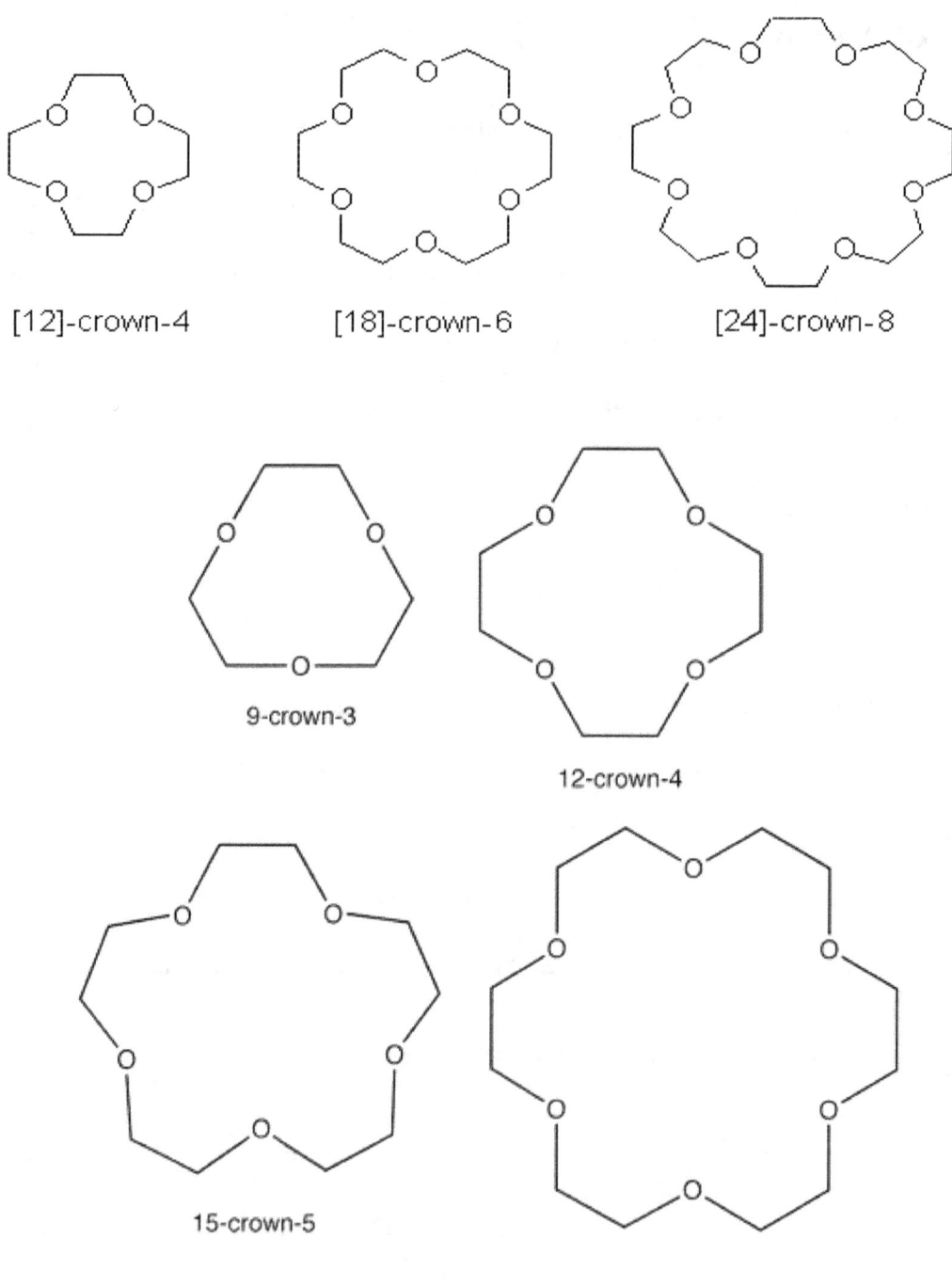

[12]-crown-4   [18]-crown-6   [24]-crown-8

9-crown-3

12-crown-4

15-crown-5

18-crown-6

Crown ether molecules can trap metal ions by forming ion-dipole bonds with them, resulting in an entity known as host-guest complex, in which the crown

ether molecule is the host and the metal ion is the guest.

eg:

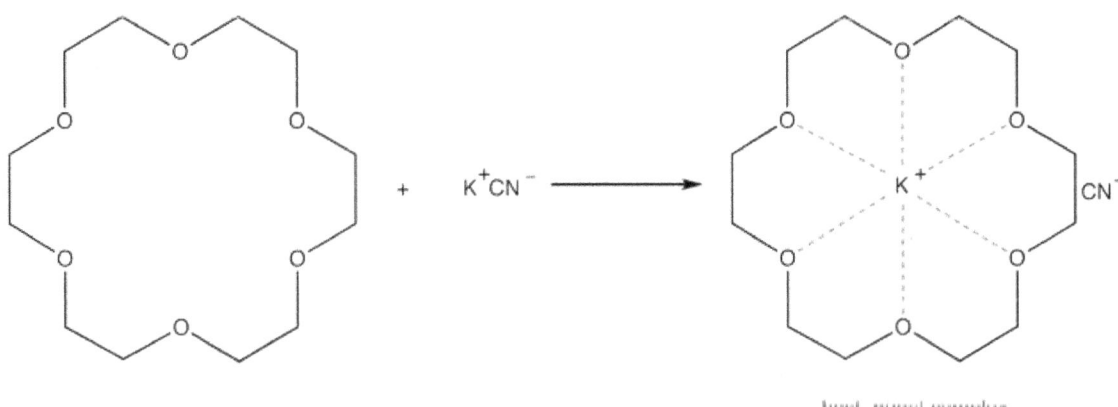

host-guest complex

Since the diameter of the cavity of a crown ether molecule is more or less a

constant, the ability of a crown ether molecule to form a stable host-guest

complex with a metal ion is highly selective.

eg:

cavity diameter: 18–crown–6 > 15–crown–5

ionic radius; K+ > Na+

18–crown–6 makes a stable host-guest complex with K+ (1), but not with Na+,

whereas 15–crown–5 makes a stable host-guest complex with Na+ (2), but not

with K+.

133

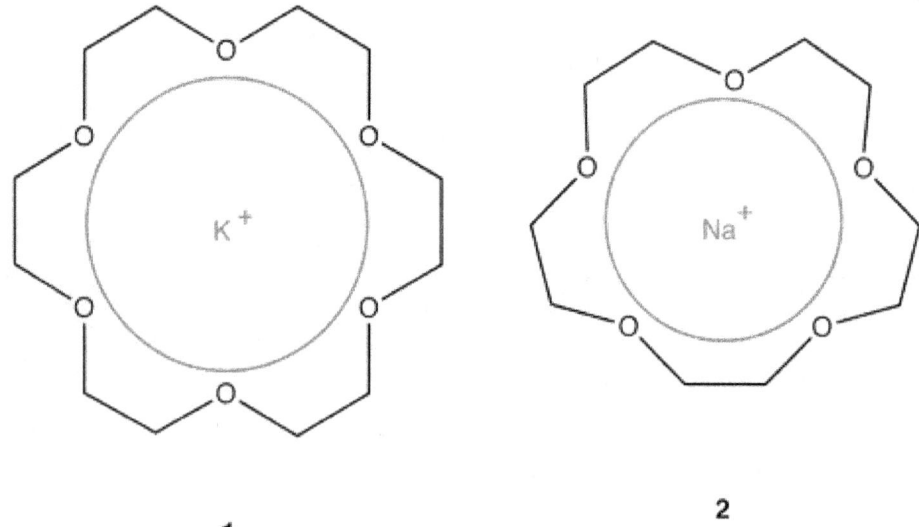

1

2

Merrifield Resin

Merrifield Resin is the common name for chloromethylated polystyrene crosslinked with 1-2% divinylbenzene (DVB). It is named for the Nobel prize-winning chemist Bruce Merrifield who popularized its use in solid phase peptide synthesis. It remains one of the popular resins for Boc based peptide synthesis. Compounds are attached through nucleophilic displacement of the chlorine atom. Finished peptides are commonly cleaved with hydrofluoric acid (HF), but trifluoromethanesulfonic acid (TFMSA) or trimethylsilyl trifluoromethansulfonate (TMSOTf) can be used instead. Because it is somewhat acid labile, Merrifield resin is not recommended for synthesizing very large peptides. It is is the starting material for a diverse assortment of modified resins. By attaching different linkers, a wide variety of resins with special applications have been produced.

PETERSON OLEFINATION

The Peterson Reaction allows the preparation of alkenes from α-silylcarbanions. The intermediate β-hydroxy silane may be isolated, and the elimination step - the Peterson Elimination - can be performed later. As the outcome of acid or base-induced elimination is different, the Peterson Olefination offers the possibility of improving the yield of the desired alkene stereoisomer by careful separation of the two diastereomeric β-hydroxy silanes and subsequently performing two different eliminations.

137

The Peterson olefination is the chemical reaction of α-silyl carbanions 1 with ketones(or aldehydes) to form a β-hydroxysilane 2 which eliminates to form alkenes 3.

Mechanism of the Peterson Olefination

138

Acidic hydrolysis proceeds via an anti-elimination:

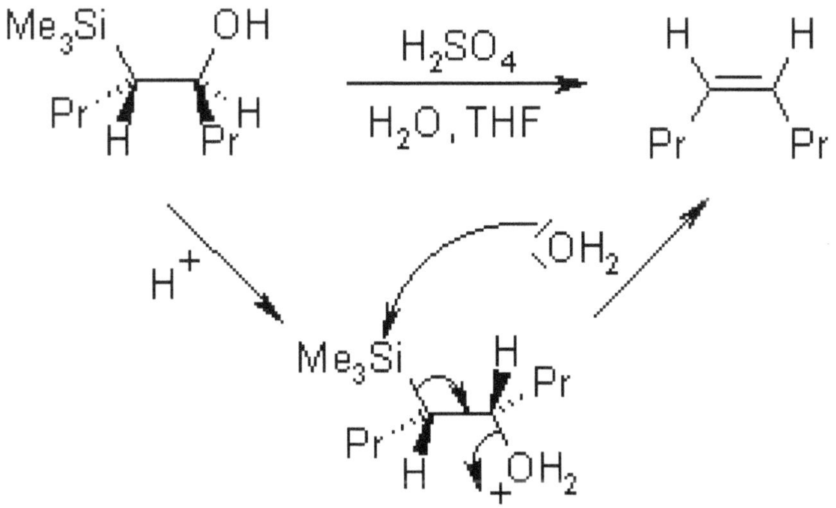

In contrast, the base-catalyzed elimination may proceed via a 1,3-shift of the silyl group after deprotonation, or with the formation of a pentacoordinate 1,2-oxasiletanide that subsequently undergoes cycloreversion:

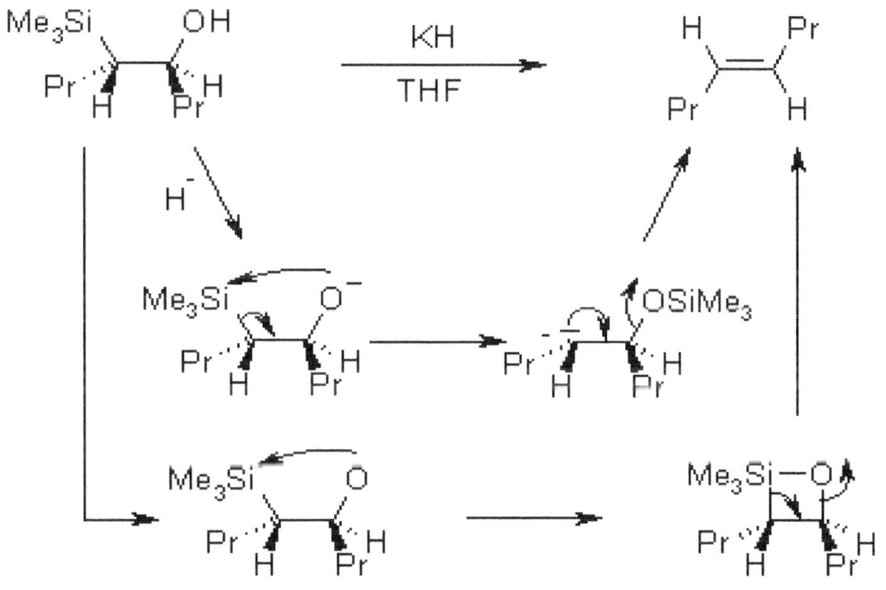

The use of α-silyl organomagnesium compounds is helpful for the isolation of the intermediate β-hydroxysilanes, because magnesium strongly binds with oxygen, making the immediate elimination impossible. If excess organolithium or lithium amide base is used to generate the α-silyl carbanion, this base can effect the deprotonation as well, and since the lithium-oxygen bond is not as strong as magnesium-oxygen, the reaction leads directly to the alkene. Some reactions proceed with good diastereoselectivity, so the direct conversion can be an attractive option.

The Peterson reaction is stereospecific. This is because it is an *E2*-elimination proceeding via an *anti-periplanar* transition state. In principle, it can therefore be used to make single geometrical isomers of alkenes, with the geometry depending on the relative stereochemistry of the starting material

The elimination step of the Peterson reaction can be conducted under either acidic or basic conditions, and in each case the reaction is stereospecific. Thus a single diastereoisomer of the starting β-hydroxysilane gives a single isomer of the alkene.

erythro diastereoisomer

(E)

threo diastereoisomer

(Z)

Mechanism - acidic conditions

anti conformation

Mechanism - basic conditions

syn conformation

142

WILKINSON CATALYST

$$Ph_3P-Rh\begin{smallmatrix}\cdots PPh_3\\\\-Cl\\Ph_3P\end{smallmatrix}$$

WILKINSON CATALYST

RhCl(PPh$_3$)$_3$ - Chlorotris(triphenylphosphine)rhodium(I), is known as Wilkinson's catalyst. It is used as a homogeneous hydrogenation catalyst. It is a square planar 16-electron complex. The oxidation state of Rhodium in it is +1.

It is used in the selective hydrogenation of alkenes and alkynes without affecting the functional groups like: C=O, CN, NO$_2$, Aryl, CO$_2$R etc.

Initially, the catalyst activates the molecular dihydrogen by oxidative addition mechanism to give a 18 valence electron dihydrido complex. The oxidation state of Rh is increased to +3. Thus formed dihydrido complex binds to the olefin in the next step with the concomitant loss of solvent or PPh$_3$ ligand. Since the activation of dihydrogen occurs before addition of olefin, this path is referred to as dihydride path. Now one of the hydrogen undergoes migratory insertion at the double bond. This is a slow step i.e., Rate Determining Step (RDS).Immediately and finally, the alkane is released rapidly by an irreversible reductive elimination step that completes the catalytic cycle.

The oxidation state of Rh is decreased to +1 and the catalyst is regenerated.

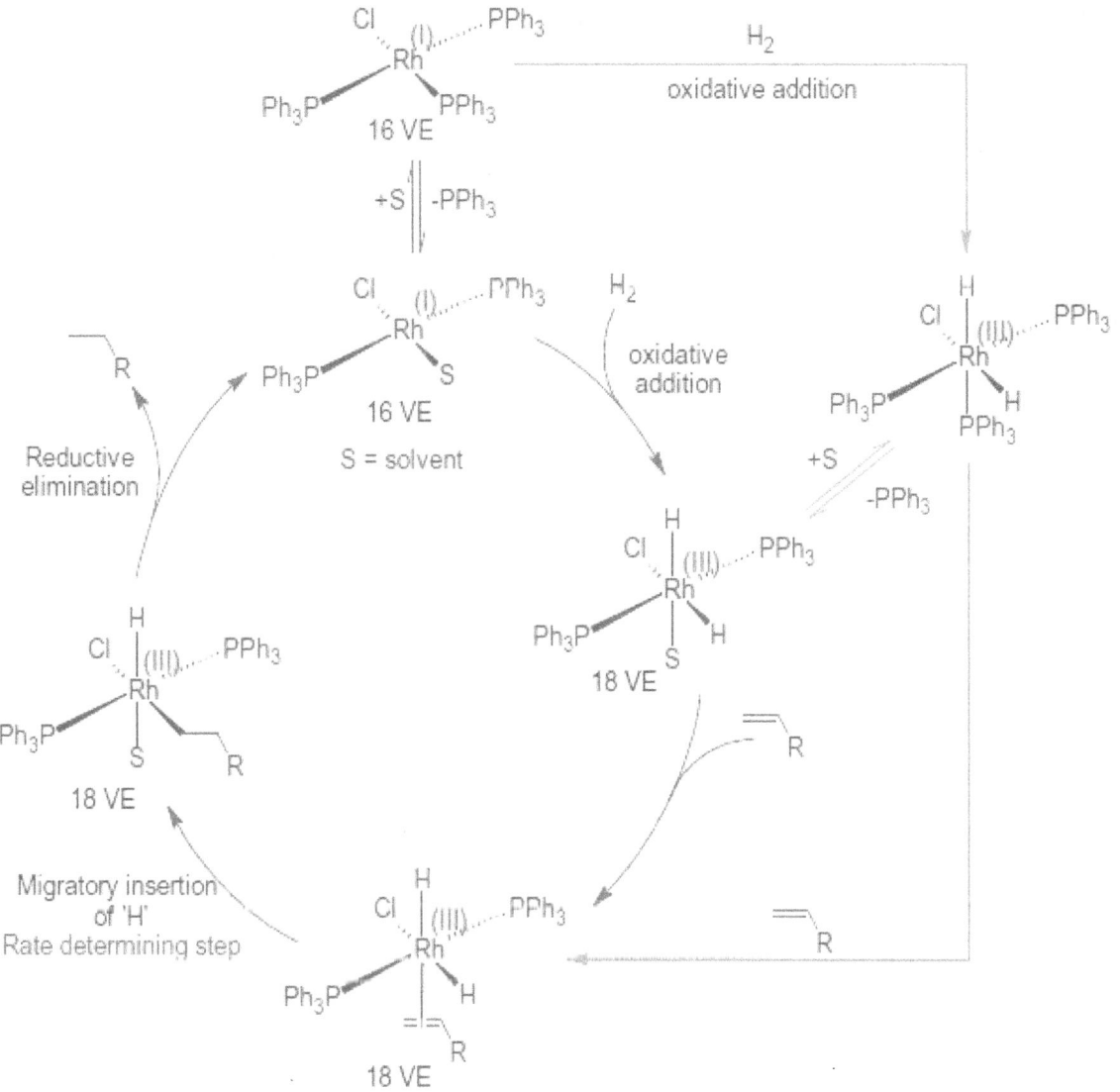

Less substituted and sterically less hindered double bonds are selectively hydrogenated.

Exocyclic double bonds are selectively hydrogenated over endocyclic double bonds.

Cis alkenes are reduced rapidly than trans alkenes.

Isolated double bonds are rapidly hydrogenated over conjugated dienes.

$$\text{RhCl(PPh}_3)_3$$
$$\xrightarrow{\text{H}_2\text{, benzene}}$$

Terminal alkynes are hydrogenated more rapidly than terminal alkenes.

$$\text{RhCl(PPh}_3)_3$$
$$\xrightarrow{\substack{\text{H}_2\text{, benzene} \\ \text{2,2,2-Trifluoroethanol}}}$$

Unsaturated substrates containing polar functionality are hydrogenated more rapidly.

$$\text{RhCl(PPh}_3)_3$$
$$\xrightarrow{\text{H}_2\text{, benzene}}$$

Hydrogenations catalyzed by Wilkinson's catalyst involve stereospecific syn hydrometallation of the multiple bond followed by stereospecific reductive elimination. Hence the hydrogenation of olefins or alkynes result in syn addition products.

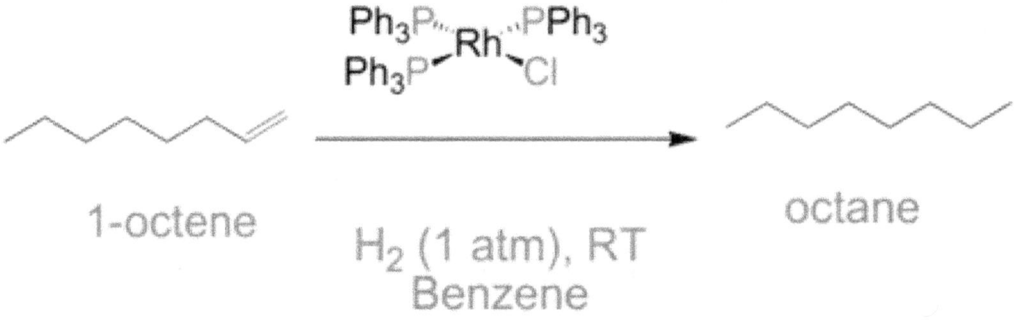

1-octene → octane

Ph₃P""Rh""PPh₃ / Ph₃P—Rh—Cl

H₂ (1 atm), RT
Benzene

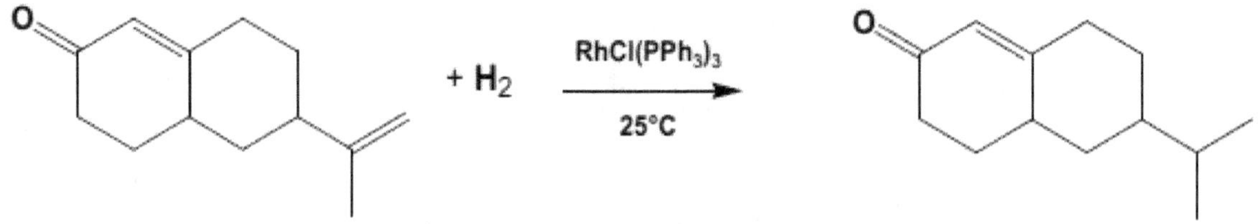

+ H₂ → RhCl(PPh₃)₃, 25°C

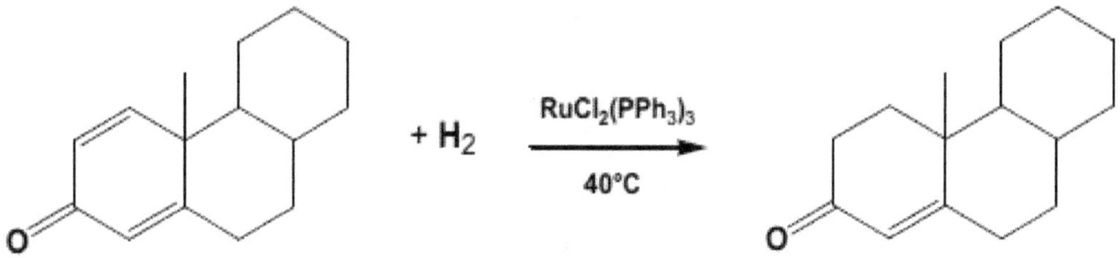

+ H₂ → RuCl₂(PPh₃)₃, 40°C

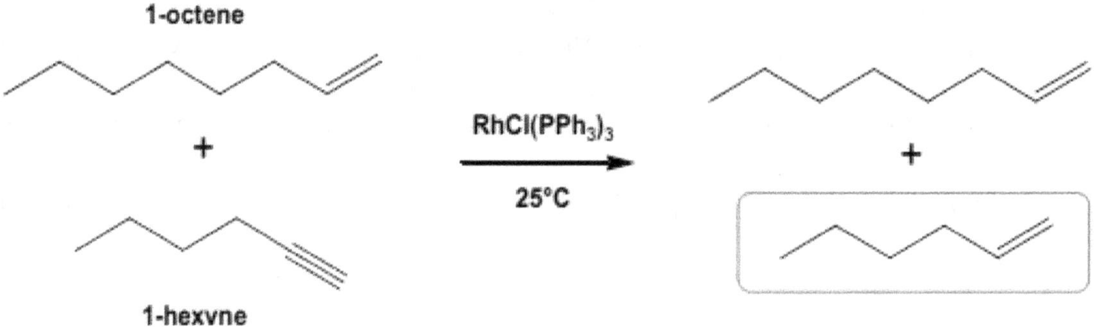

1-octene

+

1-hexyne

RhCl(PPh₃)₃, 25°C →

+

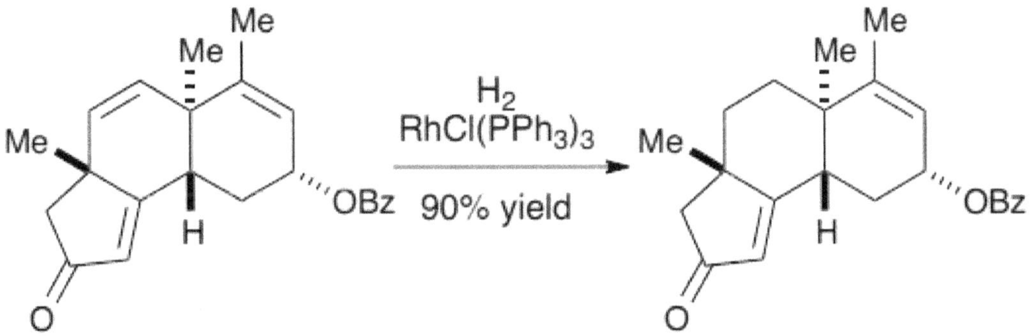

Reaction 1:

H_2
RhCl(PPh$_3$)$_3$
90% yield

Me, Me, Me, Me, OBz, O, H

→

Me, Me, Me, Me, OBz, O, H

Reaction 2:

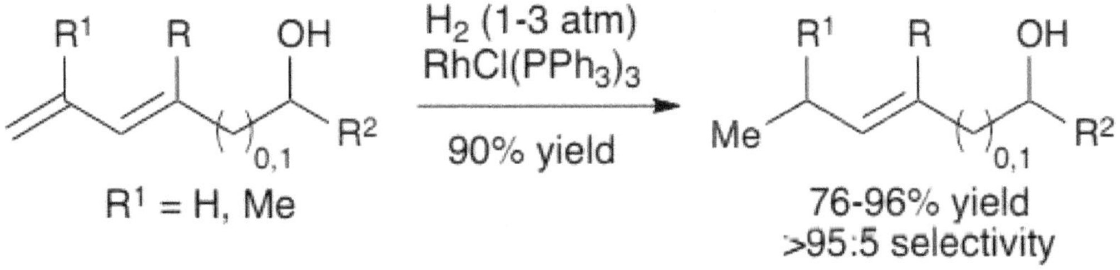

R^1 R OH
R^2
0,1
R^1 = H, Me

H_2 (1-3 atm)
RhCl(PPh$_3$)$_3$
90% yield

→

R^1 R OH
Me R^2
0,1
76-96% yield
>95:5 selectivity

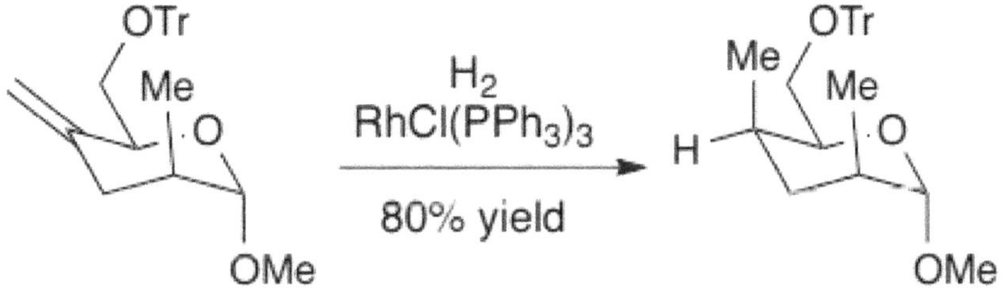

Reaction 3:

OTr
Me
O
OMe

H_2
RhCl(PPh$_3$)$_3$
80% yield

→

OTr
Me Me
H O
OMe

BAKER'S YEAST

Bakers yeast is a commercial preparation consisting of dried cells of one or more strains of the fungus Saccharomyces cerevisiae, used as a leavening in baking. The word "yeast" comes from the Sanskrit 'yas' meaning "to seethe or boil". Yeast is a living microscopic organism which converts sugar or starch into alcohol and carbon dioxide, which is why beer brewers, wine makers and bread bakers like it. Baker's yeast is the common name for the strains of yeast commonly used as a leavening agent in baking bread and bakery products, where it converts the fermentable sugars present in the dough into carbon dioxide and ethanol.

Baker's yeast is what we use most often for leavening when cooking. Baker's yeast is either active dry yeast (where the yeast is alive but inactive due to lack of moisture) or compressed fresh yeast (where the yeast is alive and extremely perishable as a result). Brewer's yeast is a non-leavening yeast used in brewing beer and can be eaten as a food supplement for its healthful properties (as you would wheat germ), unlike baker's yeast which is used for leavening. Brewer's years has a bitter hops flavor.

Baker's yeast is of the species *Saccharomyces cerevisiae*, which is the same species commonly used in alcoholic fermentation, which is called Brewer's Yeast.

Saccharomyces cerevisiae is known as top-fermenting yeast. It is one of the major types of yeast used in the brewing of beer so called because during the fermentation process it rises to top of the fermentation vessel. Beers that use top-fermenting yeast are called ales, and for that reason these yeasts are also sometimes called "ale yeasts".

Baker's yeast is also a single-cell microorganism found on and around the human body.

Uses:

- Asymmetric reduction of a wide variety of ketones into alcohol (–CHOH) group

- Reduction of double bond

Ex 1

Ex 2

Ex 3

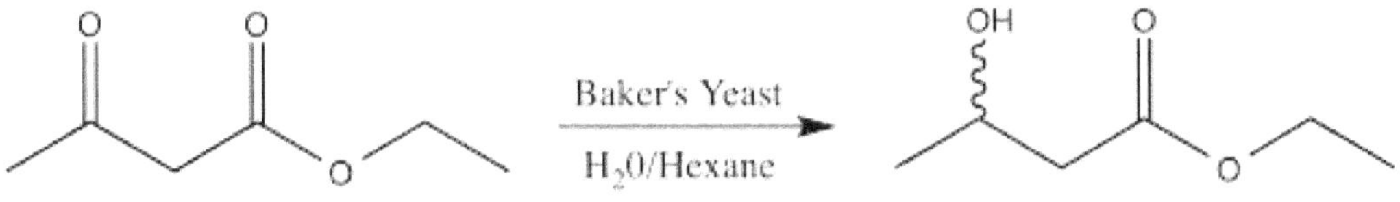

ethyl acetoacetate

Ex 4

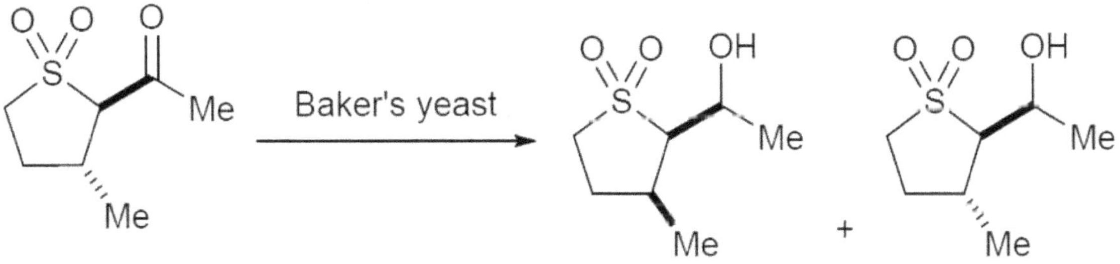

Ex 5

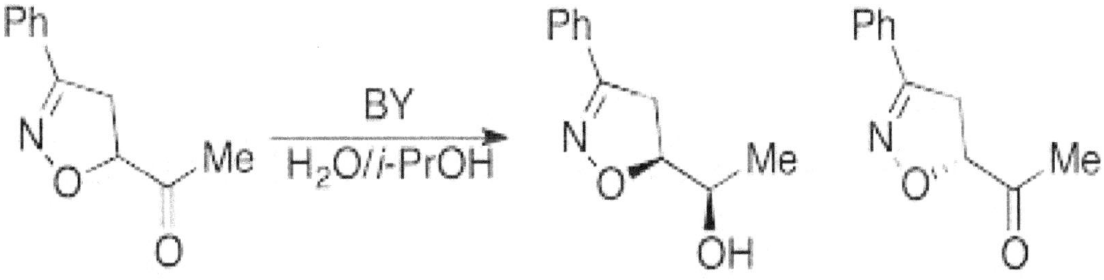

99% ee   98% ee

Ex 6

Ex 7

Ex 8

(1R,3S)-anti
ee = 98%

(1S,3S)-syn
ee 97%

Ex 9

(2S,4R)-anti
single diastereoisomer
ee = 99%, yield 23%

Ex 10

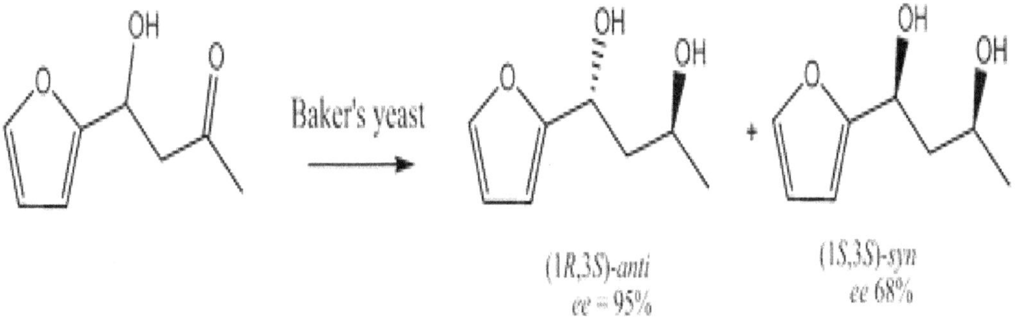

Baker's yeast

(1R,3S)-anti
ee = 95%

(1S,3S)-syn
ee 68%

Ex 11

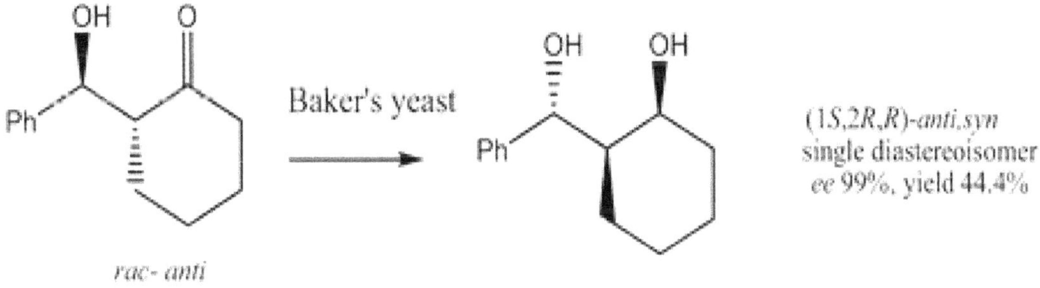

OH

Ph

Baker's yeast

OH   OH

Ph

(1S,2R,R)-anti,syn
single diastereoisomer
ee 99%, yield 44.4%

rac- anti

Ex 12

OMe   O

R   OEt

Baker's yeast

OMe   O

R   OEt

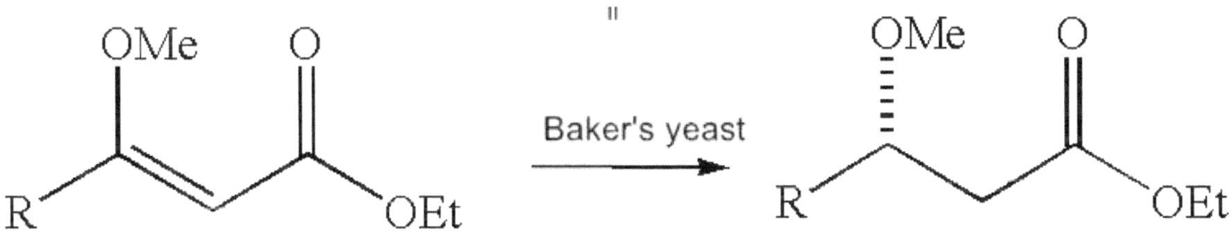

Ex 13

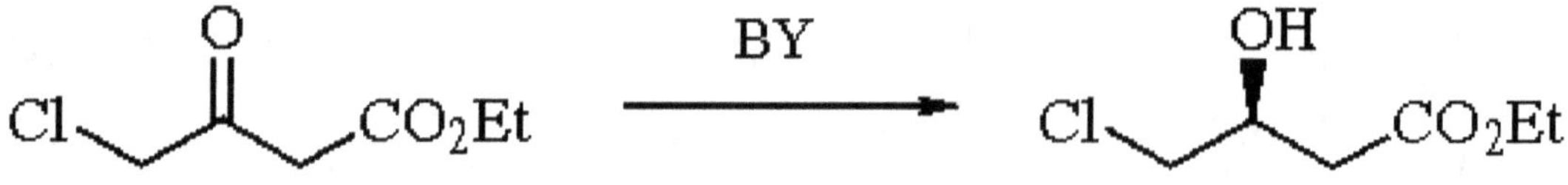

(*S*)
55% ee

Ex 14

Ex 15

Ex 16

Ex 17

(S)
84-87% ee

www.ingramcontent.com/pod-product-compliance
Lightning Source LLC
Chambersburg PA
CBHW080412290526
45791CB00008BA/2249

www.ingramcontent.com/pod-product-compliance
Lightning Source LLC
Chambersburg PA
CBHW080412290526
45791CB00008BA/2249